TEENAGERS AND PARENTS:

Ten Steps For A Better Relationship

by

Roger McIntire and Carol McIntire

McIntire, Roger W., 1935-
    Teenagers and parents : ten steps for a better relationship / by
Roger McIntire and Carol McIntire. -- Columbia, MD : Summit
Crossroads Press, 1995.
    p. cm.
    Includes bibliographical references and index.
    Originally published: Amherst, Mass. : HRD Press, 1991.
    ISBN 0-9640558-4-8

    1. Parent and teenager--United States.   2. Adolescent psychology
--United States.   I. McIntire, Carol.   II. Title.

HQ799.15.M15 1995   649'.125
                                           QBI95-20111

Copyright 1994 by
        Summit Crossroads Press
        11065 Swansfield Road
        Columbia, MD 21044-2709
        1-800-362-0985, 1-410-740-6920

First Edition, 1991
Second Edition, 1995

ISBN #0-9640558-4-8

Illustrations by George Phillips
Cover Design by Old Mill Graphics
Production Services by Susan Kotzin

About the Authors

Roger and Carol McIntire have worked with families and their teenagers for many years and have three grown daughters of their own. Roger retired as Professor of Psychology after 32 years at the University of Maryland where he also served as Associate Dean. He has been a consultant and teacher of teachers in grade schools, high schools and colleges and has published research concerning infant vocalizations, eating problems, strategies in elementary and high schools, and college retention.

Carol was recognized for her expertise in working with difficult children and children with special needs. She worked with students and their parents in both middle and high schools from 1974 until her death in 1990. Among her accomplishments was the establishment of a highly successful program for paying high school students to tutor middle schoolers.

Roger McIntire has written several other books including *For Love of Children* (Psychology Today) and *Child Psychology* (Behaviordelia). His latest book, *Enjoy Successful Parenting* (Summit Crossroads Press) is for parents of children ages 2 to 10.

TABLE OF CONTENTS

PREFACE
Raising a Teenager to Be an Adult, While Keeping a Friend

How did you get safely through the family dinner conversation when you were a teenager? What did you say when Mom asked, "What did you do at school today?" Maybe you remember Mom's question as an opening to a safe conversation about your day. Perhaps Mom always seemed interested and on your side, without looking for your mistakes. Or maybe you answered, "Not much," because your past experience with Mom's habits told you that the question would lead to criticism of your behavior. Possibly it was best to keep it short because of the likelihood of correction. Either way, Mom's likely reactions molded your conversational strategy. Today, your teenager will do and say things at home that are adjustments to your conversational habits. Each of us has seen parents who react in ways that signal encouragement, or in ways that produce a quiet, non-cooperative attitude.

Your reactions can keep conversations in an agreeable mode without slipping into negative reactions that shut down conversation. Agreeable conversation will ease the way for the other steps toward improving school and social behaviors and guide teens to become adults. Starting today, your attention to your style of conversation can smooth out the family airways. The steps that follow take up specific teen behaviors and parent strategies.

The steps will influence your teen toward a better direction in life and a better attitude. And, in addition, the steps will make *your* life more pleasant. The key is to keep some long-term goals in mind while using some positive ways to handle the daily changes and

Don't overreact. Instead, ask a neutral question such as an *IT*-question and show empathy for your teen.

surprises. The ten steps will suggest a ready list of ways for raising your teen to be an adult.

There are two goals most parents have that always seem at odds with each other: "How do I get my teen to behave in the right way?" and "How do I continue our good relationship?" Putting the concern for good behavior first and the relationship second is a common and tempting pitfall. Satisfying family relationships will *lead* to good behaviors, but occasional successes in good behaviors will not, *in themselves*, lead to good parent-daughter/son relationships. In order to maintain a good relationship while also continuing some control, steps need to be followed that lead to expanding independence for teens. The steps build their self-confidence and provide opportunity for teens to practice good behavior. The steps must allow parents to praise, encourage, *and* like their teen. And, all the while, parents need to feel good about themselves and their family role in order to maintain the effort.

When you were a teenager, did you want *your* parents to know more about being better parents? If you did, you probably meant you wanted them to show how much they liked you and encourage your successes. Teens often feel that when they are good, nobody seems to notice. They think it's only when they do wrong things that parents have a lot of reactions. When you were growing up, you knew your parents *loved* you, but in your day-to-day interactions, were you always sure they *liked* you?

When you are unsure about someone liking you, pleasant conversation is difficult, disagreements become aversive, and obedience comes only when a power struggle is lost. "Children" long gone from the family nest and on their own often find themselves in this same old struggle with parents. The amount of conflict or liking in conversations lingers on after childhood and adolescence, and shows up even in adult years. We combine the topics with tone, criticism, and interest to show others how they are liked. So the first step to building a good relationship with your teenager is to use positive communication. Managing problem behaviors comes later. The goals of these ten steps are 1) to raise a teenager to become a competent adult, 2) to have all the family members enjoy the family process, and 3) for all to remain close friends when the job is done.

STEP 1
COMMUNICATE IN POSITIVE WAYS

Your style of communication sends a message. It tells the listener how you feel about him/her. A teen listening to a parent extracts this evaluation in less than a sentence. If the signals are negative, a teen puts up defensive reactions before any useful exchange begins.

"I *love* them, but I don't always *like* them and it always comes through. How can I show my teen that I like her and still show necessary disapproval?" Answer: you can't like anyone's behavior 100%, but if you can be non-critical, the greatest amount of liking and friendship comes through.

Do you like your fellow employees at work? Some of them? Possibly the ones with whom you've found "lots in common," discoveries made in easygoing conversations. It takes a lot of learning about someone to like them. Let's get started by opening up the doors in conversation. *There are some rules to this important game.*

> **TAKE ONE:** "You should have seen what happened in gym today, Dad."
>
> "What, Donald?"
>
> "Keith got in an argument with Mr. Effort and they ended up in a real fight!"
>
> "I'm sure it wasn't much of a fight."
>
> "Yes it was! They were wrestling!"
>
> "I hope you didn't have anything to do with it."
>
> "Naw, all I did was cheer."
>
> "Cheer? Listen, Donald, you'll end up in trouble right along with Keith! Don't you have any more sense than to...."

Let's interrupt Dad here just for a moment. Donald, like all teens, resents the way his dad turned his story into a talk about the mistakes that Donald might have made. The experience will limit his talks with Dad in the future. Dad criticized his son's story: (1) he thinks Donald was wrong because it wasn't much of a fight, (2) Donald probably had something to do with it, and (3) he shouldn't have cheered. Dad centered the conversation on what he disliked about his son's behavior instead of the story. All this happened in a twenty-second discussion. *Our first rule of conversation is to avoid instant criticism.* Let's back up and give Dad another chance to be more friendly but help Donald consider possible consequences of the gym-class experience.

   RETAKE: "You should have seen what happened in gym today, Dad."

   "What happened, Donald?"

   "Keith got in an argument with Mr. Effort and they ended up in a real fight!"

   "How did it all start?" (Dad ignores the possible exaggeration, doesn't express doubt, and shows interest instead.)

   "They just started arguing about the exercises and Keith wouldn't give in."

   "Hard to win against the teacher." (Dad comments in general, and suggests alternatives not directly critical of Donald.)

   "Yeah, Keith is in big trouble."

   "Did they ever get around to the exercises?" (Dad is interested in the story, not just in making points and giving advice.)

   "Keith was sent to the office and then we tried these safety belts for the flips. Do you know about those?"

   "I don't think we had them in my school."

   "Well, you have these ropes..."

   Donald has a clearer view of the incident now, and understands the hopelessness of Keith's argumentative attitude. He wasn't distracted with defending himself when he told Dad the story. And now he's explaining something to his father; Dad is showing respect for Donald and seems to think Donald has something interesting to say.

Teens Dislike Evaluation. Immature people are usually self-centered. Some adults and almost all teens fit this category. The most important part of conversation for these people is, "What does the message say about *me?"* Young people "tune in" to the parts of conversations—the parts about them, and they are less interested in the *content* of talks. The teen reacts to opinions expressed about him or her while *we thought the topics were the important part!* So your teens may learn that all conversations with you are safe, because you never bring up their shortcomings and failures. Or teens may learn that you always have a criticism, and little talks with you should be avoided.

Use "It" instead of "You." People who use positive communication are "easy to talk to." They seem interested in the other person (they talk about, and ask about the other person). If conversation becomes threatening, they make it comfortable for the teenager by using the second rule of conversation: *try to look at a problem as an "it" instead of "you" or "me."*

TAKE ONE: Parent: "How was art class today?"

"Oh, O.K., what I saw of it."

"What do you mean?"

"Mrs. Clay sent me to the office."

"What did you do?"

"I didn't do anything!"

"You must have done something; you aren't sent to the office for nothing!"

"You never think it could be the teacher's fault; you always blame me!"

"What kind of talk is that? Let's have the whole story!"

"Oh, nuts!" (Teen stomps out.)

We can do better by keeping the personal threat at a low level and using "IT" statements instead.

RETAKE: "How was art class today?"

"Oh, O.K., what I saw of it."

"What do you mean?"

"Mrs. Clay sent me to the office."

"WHAT happened?" (Emphasize "it" rather than "you." *IT* happened. This is much better than, "What did *YOU* do?")

"Tom ripped my paper."

"Oh no!" (Emphasize sympathy rather than a mistake.)

"Yeah, so I shoved him."

"And so she sent you to the office?" (Emphasize the punishment without adding to it.)

"Yeah."

"Then what happened?"

"Well, for one thing, I'm behind in art again."

"Well, if you can stay away from Tom maybe you'll catch up. What else happened today?" (Add a little parental advice and then on to looking for someTHING more positive.)

Use Reflective and Sympathetic Statements. Often a teen's first remarks are only an expression of feelings and are short on facts. If a parent reacts with advice or opinion with so little information, the parent's response could be way off target. Reflective statements are useful to hear the teen out. The term, reflective, describes parental reactions that say nothing new but only reflect (repeat) what the teen said. They keep the conversation going, and provide opportunities to get straightforward information, without defensiveness. They repeat what the first speaker said while they also show sympathetic understanding. Let's look at an example of reflective statements in action by a father learning about his daughter.

"Man, is that school boring!"

Dad says, "It's really getting you down." (He just uses different words for "boring"; this is reflective, and sympathetic.)

"You bet."

"What's getting you the most?" (A good "it"-question starts with "what," instead of, "Why are *YOU* so bored?")

"I don't know. I guess it's the whole thing."

"You need a break." [Good, sympathetic remark that avoids, "There must be something wrong (with you)!" which would be threatening.]

"Yeah, but vacation is six weeks away."

"Got any plans?" (Good, this puts the conversation on a positive topic.)

"No."

"Hard to think that far ahead." (This is a reflective statement that repeats "No plan" in different words; it is also sympathetic and friendly.)

"Pam is getting some applications for camps."

"Sounds like a good idea."

"I might ask her about it."

A complaint about boredom such as this is a familiar remark to most parents. Although not much is solved about boredom in this conversation, Dad has a better understanding of the feelings of his

Don't blame teen or suggest solutions. Instead, pay attention, keep eye contact and reflect what teen says.

Be available to listen and reflect teen's words and feelings.

daughter and may find a greater strength for tolerance. He avoided the temptation to "get something done" in this short talk. Indirectly, Dad said he has had similar feelings to his daughter's and it's all right to have those. Most important, it's all right to talk to Dad about feelings because you will not be criticized for feeling "bored". Since Dad has allowed his daughter to direct the topic, information has flowed to him. He now has a "ticket of admission" to begin next time.

"Say, did Pam ever get any camp applications?" or,
"Only five weeks to go now; how's it going?"

A few weeks and months of this effort from Dad and these two will be good friends. Notice there is no room for "old chestnuts" in this approach. "Old chestnuts" such as, "You're always sloppy!" "You never do your homework!" and "You have bad friends!" shouldn't come up. Such criticisms are too broad, and therefore, will be taken personally. There's no room for "old chestnuts" in

Avoid solution suggestions. Instead, show empathy.

Step 1. Instead, the teen is encouraged to take the conversational lead and parental topics are postponed. The other steps in this book will deal with old chestnuts.

Practice this approach with your teen: (1) avoid criticism; (2) keep the conversation in a third-person form, not a discussion of her/him, nor a discussion of you; (3) use questions frequently to show interest; (4) respond with reflective and sympathetic comments often, instead of evaluations. Evaluations only emphasize your authority (rightness) and your teen's ignorance (wrongness).

"Life is so depressing. People are so bad."

"I know it gets like that at times," Mom said. Here's a good start. It may seem like a terrible start because of the topic, but the topic is the teen's choice. A terrible start would be for Mom to disagree right away with the teenager by giving a solution such as, "You shouldn't talk like that; there are a lot of good people in the world!" It would be tempting to make this correction immediately but it's unnecessary—he knows his remark is extreme. Also it's dishonest on Mom's part because she knows he's partly right. Since it's a statement with some potential for agreement, Mom should take the side that puts her a little closer. Let's see how it goes:

"It gets like that ALL the time at school."

"There must be some times that are good at school." Not good. It's too early in the conversation for the implied disagreement, authority, and solution expressed in this nudge. Let's take that back and try again:

"School's been bad lately, huh?" This is better because it's reflective without evaluating who's to blame; it keeps the conversation on a third entity where the teen started it (not his fault; not Mom's). The next remark from the teen is likely to be informative about what the problem is at school; the parent, if careful, will learn a great deal and the teen will have a chance to "get it all out."

In most conversations between adults, the suggestions for solutions are left out completely. We don't end a conversation with a neighbor, "So we're agreed you'll cut the hedge at least every two weeks!" or, "So don't go roaring off in your car like that. It disturbs everyone!" If those statements are familiar, you probably don't see much of your neighbors!

Be satisfied that most conversations with your teen, like those with your neighbor, will have little immediate result. Leave out the closing comment in most of your conversations. If you try to be the "winner" in every talk, then you will always have to make a "loser."

Use TV's Content. Teens and parents need variety from the daily routine and repetitious discussion topics: friends, school, and hobbies. When Mom and Dad make separate lists of topics they discuss with their teenager, TV programs come up often. Parents may see TV as an intruder to parental influence, but it can be a rich source of neutral, lively subjects for conversation, especially when adults and teens watch together.

Help a Teen Explore Alternatives. Reflecting a teen's statements can help the teenager get to a point of exploring alternatives and taking action to solve a problem. When a parent sends messages, "I heard you. It's all right to feel the way you do," it helps. Then a teenager is likely to go beyond letting out feelings to considering, "What can I do about it?" or "What would help?" A parent helps most by tuning in to the teen's level of emotions and energy for the problem.

Is the teen looking for alternatives, considering a particular one, or just letting out emotion? The parent must listen with empathy and react appropriately to give support. If the teen is getting rid of emotion, a helpful parent reflects that. Sometimes a teen hasn't figured out alternatives but wants to.

Teen: I don't know what to do!

Parent: What alternatives are there?" Teens are creative at listing options when they are ready. But if nothing comes, it may be that the problem isn't clear yet and the teen needs to explore more or just express opinions and feelings.

Perhaps a teen is ready to try an alternative.

Teen: I'm going to tell those kids to quit bugging me!

Parent: How do you think they'll react to that?

Teen: They might stop, but if they don't I'll just ignore them from now on.

Parent: Just ignore them?

Teen: Yeah, that works every time!

Distinguishing different teen levels of emotion and energy, and reacting with support requires practice and empathy from the parent. When in doubt, be reflective and use "it" questions, but resist the temptation to suggest solutions.

Suggesting Solutions. Parents are always tempted to suggest solutions to problems: "Why don't you..." "You should try..." "Don't be so..." These statements are well meaning but they often strike the listener as pushy and superior, so we need to add a **fifth** rule to the ones listed above: Use solution-oriented statements carefully, only after all of the problem has been fully expressed. As an example, look at the temptations in the following conversation.

Dad: What did you think of that show?

Lisa: The babies stole the audience! They were cute.

Dad: Never cried, or needed diaper changes.

> Lisa: Not very realistic, I guess, but I liked Grandpa talking to the twins.
>
> Dad: Babies need to hear a lot of talk to learn.

TV situations are not threatening because they happen to someone else and the teen has as much information as the parent, because they both watched the same show. Help your teen react to and question TV shows, rather than simply letting him/her be a passive viewer. You have your attitudes and answers to life's questions and TV can help your teen form his/her views, especially when there is someone to listen and ask questions.

An Exercise—Practice Communication Skills

With another parent or a friend, practice the rules of Step 1 while you share a simple story such as a shopping trip, difficulty getting the kids to school, or helping them with homework. Begin with one person as the listener and one as the teller. Master these guidelines before going on to other steps.

1. ***Keep eye contact.*** Look at your conversation partner most of the time. A teen expects a good listener to look at him/her. Adults don't like to feel unattended because the person we are trying to talk to is staring at a newspaper or TV while we ask a question. Teens feel that way, too.

2. ***Use good posture.*** Face your teen while talking and listening. Use body language that says, "I'm alert! I'm interested!" A parent who slumps, looks away, or even WALKS away sends messages that discourage and insult the talker.

3. ***Avoid criticism and ask questions.*** Use questions that continue the conversation by asking for longer answers than just "yes" or "no." "How did it feel?" is more likely to continue the talk than "What time was it?" Emphasize *IT* questions instead of using *YOU:* "How was it at school today?" not

"How did *you* do at school?" Careful questions can help in a neutral, non-opinionated way, so the speaker discovers a better understanding of what happened and why.

4. ***Avoid solution statements and use reflective statements.*** Reword the last thing your partner said to show you understand what he/she told you. "Boy, I really hate that Mr. Jones for math!" could be answered with, "He really annoys you," or "You get mad in there a lot, I guess."

   Replace the temptation to give advice or criticize. Instead, use reflections of your partner's statements. Suggestions such as "Why don't you...?" or "Have you tried...?" make the talker feel inferior, resentful, and argumentative. You will get the whole story by reflecting. Your listening helps because speakers will clarify their situations and feelings by telling themselves about it.

5. ***Share your experience***. Share stories, jokes, and experiences which helped you learn about getting along in life. Be selective and avoid stories that are too close to a sore point with your teen. If your son or daughter feels your experiences are not directed as advice to his/her specific weaknesses, the tales can be enjoyed and they will improve the relationship.

STEP 2

CHOOSE SPECIFIC BEHAVIORS YOU CAN INFLUENCE

Both good and bad teenage behaviors produce parental reactions. The balance between reactions to good and bad behaviors is likely to favor the negative ones, because we parents usually have specific ideas of what bad behavior is, while good behavior is often described in only general terms. We are quite sure what deserves criticism or punishment, but we are more vague about our positive expectations. This emphasis on the negative can lead parents to think of themselves more as police officers than as Moms and Dads.

Without specific positives to look for, parents become less positive toward their teens. Vague, supportive comments such as, "You're a good kid!" and "You're doing all right!", don't influence anything in particular. "Don't talk like that!" "Straighten up!" and "Clean up your mess!" have specific targets and may have an influence—if only for a short time.

We need to select the specific positive targets in order to avoid frequent criticism. When Dad complains that Kim was messy, he could be more helpful by deciding the specific actions he *wants* her to perform. He could say, "I want her to make her bed, put dirty clothes in the laundry hamper, pile her belongings on wall shelves, and dust and vacuum her room." Instead of accusing her of being "messy," or commenting on the whole person of his daughter, he could direct attention toward these specific actions. By focusing, he can take one step toward specific changes in the behaviors he feels are important for her to do. Also, Dad could begin to plan, when he can praise instead of bringing up the old chestnut, "you're messy" which may be interpreted as, "(I don't like you), you're messy". Dad can choose the best time to talk with Kim about the work, decide the level to expect from her at first, be ready with his approval and other rewards for her effort, and look for ways to encourage gradual improvement of her performance.

When we talk about the actions of teenagers, we often use descriptive terms to summarize our observations: "He is shy, she is rowdy." "He is hyperactive, she is lazy." These broad labels seem to describe characteristics that are within the person, beyond our influence. In fact, we can influence the characteristics once we identify them by specific behaviors. Instead of shy, we say, "Bill doesn't talk or look at people." By rowdy, we mean Shanna speaks in a loud voice and pokes people. "Hyperactive" becomes, "Reg interrupts his homework by walking around the room every few minutes." In specific terms, "lazy" breaks down to, "Julie listens to music and sleeps instead of doing her chores or homework." The task of being specific about *complaints* is not difficult. Often both parents and teachers have rules about particular mistakes.

The challenging part is in the listing of specifics on the good side. We have learned that most parents know what to reprimand but fumble with praise on only infrequent occasions. The following exercise asks for both lists—unwanted teen behaviors *and desired behaviors*. Lists of these specific teen behaviors are part of the preparation to plan specific parent reactions—negative when necessary, positive when deserved. One objective is to influence the specifics and increase the good behavior. A second objective is to send a strong message to your beloved teens that there are many things you *like* about them. The exercise will put you on the lookout to send proper messages. It shouldn't be skipped.

An Exercise to Choose Specific Behaviors

1. The first list should be the activities *you want your teenager to do.* You can generate a short list now, but for further suggestions see Steps 7 and 8 that describe behaviors which help teens become competent adults. Be sure that each item on your list is a real action—not an attitude or a word of only general description. Instead of writing, "Be more studious," list, "Spend more time reading, figuring,

writing, and doing math or social studies." It may seem a small difference, but "studious" is descriptive and does not happen at a particular moment so you cannot support it. But reading, writing, figuring, and doing other homework actually happen at particular times, so you have opportunities for support.

Avoid the word, "not" in your statements. Instead of "not act bored," write specifics you think are important such as, "Help with chores, spend time reading, or choose a recreational activity and stick to it for a half-year."

2. Next, number the actions on your list in their order of importance. The number one behavior is the one on the list you most want your teen to do, and the last item, the least important.

3. *Now make a second list of behaviors you dislike* and want to eliminate. Again avoid the word, "not" in your statements. Practice being specific: "He does not respect me," can be restated as, "He says the following bad things to me...."

When your list is complete, rank order the behaviors according to importance. Keep in mind that some behaviors you rated very low, so they deserve little attention. Some negative actions may be so far down on your list that it isn't worth the disruption to react to them at all.

4. You are ready to compare your first and second lists. Your first list should suggest new opportunities for you to let your teen know about successes. Select two from near the top of this list for special attention. Be on the lookout for them and take advantage of the opportunity.

Your second list will have some behaviors with such low priority that no reaction is justified. Select two from near the bottom of this list and be on the lookout for them. When these unimportant negative behaviors come up, control your reaction, ignore the mistakes,

Instead of general words, think of specific actions.

keep the airways clear for better stuff! The choices for parental *reactions* to bad behaviors will be discussed in Step 4.

Now that we have some specific behaviors, let's look at some reasons for teen behaviors which will show the importance of your reactions.

Why do teenagers do what they do?

Understanding the reasons behind specific actions can improve your influence over a teenager's behaviors. There are several reasons teens and other people do the things they do. There are unchangeable physical characteristics and early experiences that play important roles. Also, people adjust their behavior to achieve certain payoffs, such as self-satisfaction and enjoyment, attention from others, encouragement, and rewards. Physical limitations and early experiences are unchangeable, but we can change some of the payoffs people receive for their behaviors.

The "why" of behaviors is easy to see when we describe specific behaviors and their consequences. Instead of leading us to speculate about inherited traits and early traumas, the "why" question becomes "What happens next, after the behavior?" or "What are the consequences?" Kim throws her clothes down and Shanna misses the school bus. Then what happens? Someone else irons Kim's wrinkled clothes. Someone helps Shanna rush for the school bus. Those supports may be reasons *for* the poor behaviors. How can we extract ourselves from supporting bad behavior and having things go wrong? We will have to stop the payoff for behaviors we don't want, and support actions we do want.

Now we're ready for, "What happens next when the teen gets it *right*?" If Kim cleans up her room, Julie does her homework, or Shanna makes the bus on her own, your reaction can make or break that improvement. Positive feedback for correct behavior is especially important for teens because they need the message as well as the encouragement. They are not yet sure of the right way to act. Should they try to pick up clothes and be on time, or is that "uncool?" They lack information as well as motivation. Adults know more about the right ways to act so they need only a little encouragement from a friend, and enjoyable interaction follows. Teens need to be taught by more frequent positive reactions. For parents to get out of the conflict of supporting bad habits, they will need to pay diligent attention to the teen's little successes.

We all need support and incentives for our actions: pleasant reactions, paychecks, and awards, and of course, our own good feelings when we do things we value. Teens are still uncertain about what good behavior is, so they crave a lot of encouragement and payoffs, while adjusting to the consequences.

On many evenings at the dinner table, Taylor told funny stories from his school experiences. Family laughter and comments made him feel good, and during supper he trusted his family not to raise embarrassing questions about his school performance. Ellen got a lot of recognition during suppertime too, but it took the form of arguments with Dad. Disagreements were a habit because she received little notice for her accomplishments, and she had learned to start arguments and settle for the unpleasant attention as entertainment.

Taylor: So, John was looking the other way as he went around the corner at the end of the hall, and he ran right into Ms. Letty pushing a lab cart with crickets in a box. Boom! The crickets escaped as the cart bumped over and he said, "Oh! I'm sorry. I didn't mean to dump your crickets. I hope it doesn't *'bug'* you!"

Dad: What a story! What happened?

Taylor: John and Ms. Letty were jumping around chasing the crickets and some other students helped too, but some were yelling "Oh! Get them away! Don't touch them!" Everyone started laughing.

Ellen: I don't think it was so funny. Ms. Letty could have been hurt and so could those crickets.

Dad: Don't be a grump. It's just one of those harmless accidents that adds humor to the day.

Ellen: Big joke!

Dad: You ought to lighten up!

Since we understand that payoffs have a big influence on a teenager's behaviors, we can ask, "How can I support the actions I want from my teenager?" and "How can I get rid of behavior I don't want by removing support?" In Ellen's case, her father could listen and ask neutral questions as suggested in Step 1, rather than challenging her at the supper table. Instead of arguing, he needs to *go more than halfway* to encourage her appropriate contributions. The effort is essential to change.

When Ellen said, "I don't think it's so funny. Ms. Letty could have been hurt ...." she signaled the start for her arguing behavior. Perhaps in the previous exercise that listed behaviors, Dad could have decided in advance to control his reaction to Ellen's bad behavior, then he could have been alerted. His next comment could have focused on the neutral part of Ellen's remark. Dad could have said, "Yes, Ms. Letty could have been hurt and the crickets squished."

Ellen: Yes, and John was lucky everyone was so busy catching crickets he didn't get in big trouble. Next time maybe he'll look when he goes around corners.

Taylor: That's not funny.

Dad: Not funny, but a good idea for John.

This strategy requires close attention from Dad and that means some planning and singleing out of goals as in the exercise. The adult thoughtfulness of Dad and Mom can lead to the cure for poor teen behaviors.

Let's look at another example of specific behaviors and incentives which are related to school achievement.

Dan carried home a great report card. He put it between the pages of his social studies book to keep it protected on the way home; it had to be neat when he showed it to Mom.

"How was school today?"

"Pretty good—we got our report cards. Want to see?"

"You bet I want to see!"

Dan brought out the perfect card with a smile and Mom looked over the contents. "Up in math. Up in English. You didn't go down in anything! Really good! I bet our sessions after supper have helped. You try so hard."

Mom's support of good behavior was important and she was as encouraging as she could be of Dan's success, and her compliments must have been a motivation for him. Additional credit probably goes to the encouragement in the sessions after supper. The behavior that benefited from support was the PRESENT behavior. There were two behaviors in this story: bringing home the report card *and* doing homework. When Dan came in bringing home his card, he was encouraged and he certainly looked forward to it and everyone enjoyed it. After supper, a session will begin and Mom will continue her positive attention and focus on that other crucial behavior—doing the homework. Dan was getting help in BOTH places right were he needed it.

Poor report cards and poor homework make up another pair of behaviors. The temptation in this case is to give punishment for poor report cards, with only a hope that the punishment will "spill over" to more homework effort. Another tactic is to try punishment for both report cards and poor homework. This unhappy solution seems to be a trap for bad things getting worse. The situation requires an upbeat, positive approach. We will need specifics about homework added to the lists of the previous exercise— particularly on the positive list. Then we need an exercise to find the incentives to make things improve.

An Exercise to Find Incentives

1. List several payoffs you can use to support the behaviors chosen in the previous exercise. Here are some examples:

   - Social comments are powerful and readily available: "Son, I'm proud of your effort!" "That's my daughter! I'm writing Grandpa about your getting a 'B' on your big science test." "Your helping your brother means a lot to me."

   - Allowance based on chores a teen does.

   - For some ages, small treats are popular such as favorite foods, stickers, pencils.

   - Spend time together talking just for fun, or doing a game or activity you both enjoy.

   - Privileges can be used on a weekly basis, such as getting together with friends and using the car.

2. List your chief complaint from the first exercise in this chapter, and the payoffs for it that ought to be eliminated.

When you stop support for poor behavior, incentives and encouragement must be switched over to good behaviors. We all need those payoffs to be happy, healthy persons. If we remove them for poor behaviors, we must plug them in for other behaviors.

By practicing positive communication with Step 1 you are improving your relationship with your teenager. That good relationship is a key to improving your teen's behaviors. We try hard to please people who like us because we don't want to let them down. From Step 2 you are able to identify specific actions you want your teen to learn, and you can plan supports and incentives for those actions. Next, let's find realistic starting levels for new behaviors you feel are important.

STEP 3

BE REALISTIC ABOUT WHAT YOUR TEEN CAN DO

One father told about his success in changing his expectations this way: "I've always felt I just didn't know where to start with Frank. There were always so many things he did wrong!"

"So what did you work on first?" I asked.

"Everything, I guess—all his mistakes. Whenever I had the chance I went after something. But later, when the 'shotgun' approach didn't work, I sharpened my focus and lowered my expectations. I took your advice and tried to *catch him being good,* doing some little thing right. When I was realistic about what Frank might do RIGHT, today, he improved and we got along better, too!"

Start at a Level You Can Encourage. The key here is to start at a level where you can guarantee yourself an opportunity to encourage your teen's behavior. Let's say you want your teen to help at home and talk pleasantly to a younger brother or sister. Watch for an incident when the teen helps or talks nicely with his sibling. Praise the behavior in a sincere way: "I noticed how you helped Duncan with his baseball mitt. Thanks."

Younger brother Duncan left his shoes in a strange place, but when he noticed they were lost, your teen told him where they were. Recognize the aid even if it was not a big act. It is a beginning and the social support for it will have a powerful effect.

If you do not notice any help or pleasant talk between the siblings, you need to suggest a small way in which it can happen. Tell your teenager to help his younger brother or sister with pumping up a tire so the bicycle can be used. Be sure to show honest praise. Until such help or pleasant talk is a habit, you will need to notice or initiate it often, and support it with appreciation.

Choose a behavior you want your teen to use. If you decide it is important to spend a longer time working on schoolwork, praise must be given for even the first small improvement in studying. It is a starting level and encouragement should come right away. As the behavior improves you can expand your expectations as we do with adults in the workplace.

What Are Realistic Expectations?

"Mom, can you help me with this patch on my jeans?"

"Sure, why don't you let me do it? It'll be faster." Oops, this is a missed opportunity. How about replacing this first reaction with a more productive one?

"Sure, you go ahead and I'll let you know when you go wrong." That's better. Now there will be practice—he won't LEARN if he doesn't DO. But negative emphasis on the possibility of being wrong certainly doesn't provide the kind of situation in which the teen can feel comfortable. Let's try to make an additional improve-ment of the chances for a positive outcome:

"Sure, let me baste it into place; then I'm sure you can handle it." Here's a good start; it sets up a situation where the son will practice with a good chance of success, and Mom has a good chance to be encouraging.

We need to carefully match a teen's capabilities, needs, and interests to the tasks parents can encourage in order to produce the best progress and the happiest experiences. Psychologists worry about our modern society forcing adult concerns on children too soon. We should not be tempted to force financial, social, or career concerns on teens too soon as a means of "growing them up." But we can gradually allow real practice with increasing responsibilities to help them grow up, and it will increase their abilities and self esteem.

An Exercise—Give Responsibilities and Independence

Take a thoughtful look at the graph on page 31 and list the responsibilities you can gradually give over to your teen: make her

Allow for practice with the right level of effort.

bed, school lunch, phone calls for her appointments; clean his room, buy school supplies, arrange rides to activities, keep a bank account, choose a summer camp.

Ask yourself, "How many other responsibilities are important for my teen to master?" Make your list and decide which one can come next.

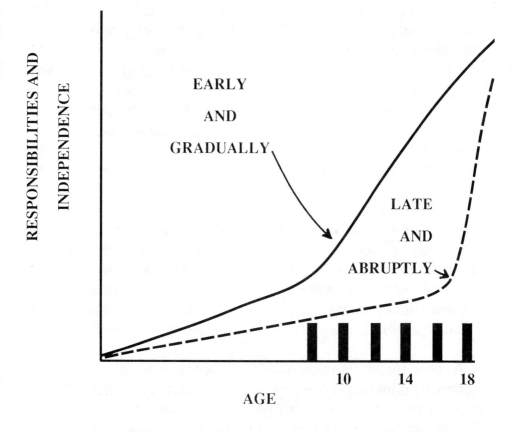

EARLY

AND

GRADUALLY

LATE

AND

ABRUPTLY

10   14   18

AGE

GIVING RESPONSIBILITIES AND INDEPENDENCE

An Exercise—Being Useful and Becoming Independent

Fill in the ages you think are appropriate for children and teens to begin taking responsibilities. At the start of each new responsibility there will be mistakes, but through practice, behaviors will be mastered before the young adult leaves home.

Responsibility	Age	Responsibility	Age
Pick up room	4	Make bed	6
Select clothes to wear	7	Bathe frequently	8
Cook meals (with help)	9	Use proper language	9
Do homework (no nagging)	10	Choose bedtime	11
Eat at meals (no comments)	11	Save and spend money (with explanation)	11
Plan and cook meals	12	Save & spend money (without explanation)	12
Buy clothes	12	Do own laundry	12
Decide hobbies & sports	13	Choose summer camp	13

Curfews:

Evening hours before 8 (with explanation)	12	Choose evening hours before 8 (no explanation)	13
Choose weekend hrs. before 10 (with explanation)	15	Choose weekend hours before 10 (no explanation)	17
Choose some weekday hours (to 10)	17	Decide limits of weekend hours (no explanation)	18

A college freshman described his lack of self-sufficiency to me. "When my parents dropped me off at the dorm, Mom was still reminding me to brush my teeth, get plenty of sleep, watch my money, and study hard. I resented it, but I also depended on her. And it's hard to keep track of everything. Nobody helps me get my bills straight; my life is nothing but lectures and books; my room is a mess and I want to quit! In a couple of days I'll be out of clean underwear anyway."

"Why don't you take your clothes to the laundry room?"

"I did, but it got fouled up. The reds turned my underwear pink!"

I tried to make a joke. "You could throw out the dirty clothes and buy all new underwear."

"I can't do that!" he said, tears starting to fill his eyes. "I don't even know my size!"

In all these years, with the size riding around with him, he still didn't know his own size! What a comment on his lack of experience in gradually learning to shop for his own things! Helping your teen to master self care and family chores will increase his/her self confidence and ability to be independent.

Tolerate Mistakes as Part of Learning. Parents will need to tolerate a teen's mistakes as an essential part of learning new behaviors. Since most errors occur when a person tries new things, it is hard to be tolerant, and parents are tempted to do things efficiently themselves; they procrastinate instead of allowing the teen new responsibilities. But if errors are seen as a part of the learning, one can be patient with errors.

Mom tolerated a half-hour of mistakes and spills to finally hear Keith say, "OK, Mom, I'm putting my cake in the oven!"

"Great. What temperature?"

"350 degrees; I'm setting it now."

"Keith, why don't you wait just a minute or two for the oven to warm. Then the outside won't be crusty from having the heat on so long at the beginning."

"Oh. That's what 'preheat' means in the recipe?"

"Right. What a treat this will be to have at supper!"

A parent can learn to tolerate the inconvenience of allowing a teen to make mistakes and improve with practice, because trying is viewed as a sign of growing to adulthood. Give responsibility now, gradually, not abruptly on the steps of a college dormitory, or in the back of a church just before a ceremony. And with each step keep the praise and incentives handy.

STEP 4

PRACTICE ALTERNATIVES
TO PUNISHMENT

Punishment comes in several forms: removing privileges, and verbal and physical reactions that cause pain of one kind or another. For a teen to grow to be a happy, independent, productive adult, the family needs to be a place where training through trial and error is encouraged and guided, the opposite of what is created when punishment is used. It is especially tempting to punish when bad behavior demands immediate reaction. When teens misbehave we must focus on long-term learning goals for them, and guard our relationship with them. But punishment doesn't deliver the needed information about what *to do.* It is not as effective or pleasant as other alternatives. We will examine the alternatives to punishment which can help you and your teenager work together. The case against punishment is strong, so let's look quickly at the many reasons against using it:

1. ***It lowers the teen's self esteem.*** The emotional put-down of punishment distracts from learning about the desired behavior. The punishment act itself is childish, and belittles the significance and power of the victim.

2. ***It hurts the parent-teenager relationship.*** Punishment tempts the teen to react to the parent with disrespect, silence, deceit, and to avoid him or her altogether whenever possible.

3. ***As punishment increases, fear inhibits practice of new behaviors.*** A high risk of punishment decreases *all teen behaviors and learning* when the parent is present, because of the atmosphere of criticism and threat.

4. ***Punishment causes a power struggle among all family members.*** It ruins the family as a nurturing place where learning is encouraged through practice and mistakes. The parent may win the struggle, but for every winner a loser is made.

5. *It makes the parent a poor role model for imitation.* The parent becomes a punisher, inflicting threats and pain. The most natural reflex to punishment is to give out some. If it is not possible to punish the parent, the teen will turn to other family members.

6. *It encourages stressful behaviors* such as nail-biting, hair-pulling, and "safer obsessions" with video games, music, and TV. Whenever encouragement and reward are low, these stress behaviors will increase. These "escapes" are very stubborn habits, maintained by their success of avoiding contact with the punisher altogether.

7. *It interferes with future negotiations.* Why negotiate if you've already paid the price of punishment in the past and expect the same in the future?

8. *It is frequently inappropriate,* not related to the behavior, which hinders learning. Most punishment is given because the *parents* have reached their limit of frustration and accumulated disappointments. A teen can better predict punishment by watching the parents' emotions than by respecting agreements. Instead of controlling his own behavior, the teen ends up tuning in to the parents' behavior!

9. *One-shot punishments cause resentment and inhibit behaviors.* These severe punishments, such as cancelling a trip or party, come too late and they produce the most resentment and argument, and the least amount of change. Instead, use small, logical, repeatable consequences which produce gradual changes in behaviors.

10. *It leads to the ultimate punishment—divorce. We refer to divorce of parent from teen.* Any teen being punished has in mind one thought, "Get away!" The teen could think of running away or just some means of withdrawing since running away is usually impractical. A phrase most hated by

teenagers is, "As long as you live in this house...." Regardless of how huffy the teen is, leaving the nest is a basic and frightening experience. Teens' emotions are thrown into conflict by thoughts of running away from punishment and parents' threats of separation. Complain as they might, your home is their most important source of security. *So don't talk about divorcing your children.* This ultimate consequence is too disturbing and implies that your value of your teen can be easily traded away. Your love and loyalty have a higher price tag and should not become part of bargaining. Instead, use the following alternatives listed below.

As you recognize how damaging punishment can be to your relationship with your teenager and to learning, alternatives take on great importance because they give you, your teenager, and your family, solutions that are effective without eroding the family. These alternatives maintain a pleasant home-life atmosphere while shaping desired behaviors. The alternatives are *ignoring, modeling, "catch 'em being good," making amends, time out,* and *making rules together.*

Ignoring means consistently overlooking relatively unimportant, undesirable behaviors and paying attention to other aspects of a teen's actions. When Tim wore a lot of oil on his hair, his parents felt it was within his personal grooming choices to do so, but when he slapped his younger sister, they reacted strongly. Their different reactions to these very different behaviors keeps the family atmosphere from becoming cluttered with more than the necessary criticism. When you react to a behavior of your teen, keep the overall family atmosphere in mind. Sacrifice family atmosphere only when necessary. For Step 2 you listed unwanted behaviors and rank ordered them. If an action takes a low priority rating, it doesn't deserve your time and energy, nor a lot of family disruption.

You may want to ignore behaviors that occur only occasionally, as well as others which come under the teen's growing sphere of control, for example: keeping a messy bedroom, using poor grammar, wearing strange outfits and unusual hairstyles. The parent's greatest influences on these daily habits will not be by way of arguments and consequences, but by way of the model the parents present. Some behaviors are part of passing stages that will be outgrown and, therefore, easier to ignore. When your teen invites a friend to visit, the bedroom will be spruced up. Unwanted grammar, language, clothing, and hairstyles are probably temporary, fluctuating with peer and media influences.

One thirteen-year-old sprayed her hair to stand up six inches above her forehead, and wore glaring makeup, but she was a good student with pleasant social skills, a tribute to her parents' ability to overlook extremes of grooming and focus instead on her *important* actions. Extremes of personal care will probably change toward the norm when the teenager wants to impress someone or get a first job.

When you ignore a behavior it can be heartening to remember that your criticism of your teen's choices would likely be viewed as attention that is *rewarding*. Escalating unusual behaviors can become an adventure when parents consistently give recognition to behaviors that deserve to be ignored. Also, focus on the benefits of ignoring—finding behaviors to which you can react positively.

While ignoring low priority, unwanted actions, increase your praise and encouragements for desired behaviors of your teen. Make the message clear: I like you; I think you're special! "I liked hearing about your report of the Civil War battle. You're learning about interesting things." "I noticed you helped clear the table after supper. That made me feel good."

Modeling always influences your teen's behavior by the example of your actions. Young adults make a lot of mistakes,

One case against punishment: teen will model parent.

being led into errors by peers, forgetting chores and commitments, indulging in unhealthy foods, wasting money and time, to mention a few. When parents see so many errors it's difficult to be accepting and look to the long-run. Instead of trying to run the teenager's life, it helps to think of the power modeling has. Temporary outside influences will not outweigh years of parental examples to make long-lasting changes in the teen's behavior. If parents have demonstrated love of education by constantly learning new things and sharing that excitement with a child, a teen is programmed to study in spite of some distractions by friends.

The effects of modeling should not be underestimated. The conversation of the moment may mislead parents to think they have no influence through modeling. But most school teachers will tell you that they are amazed at the similarities between the students and their respective parents. Parents are the constant models for their sons and daughters. If we want them to respect us, speaking and acting in ways that show consideration for their needs and capabilities will produce respect in return.

Both parent modeling and family modeling help a young person keep direction. Mom said, "In the Weiler family we try to think of and respect everyone in the family *and* outside. I expect you to live up to the Weiler standard." Of course Mom's actions must follow her words. Family sayings get across things the parents consider important. A father was fond of saying, "With all thy getting, get understanding."

The following examples show how modeling and positive consequences work together. A parent who wanted a teen to read books turned off the TV and began reading an exciting adventure novel aloud with the youngster. A mother who wants her daughter to be honest can ask, "Whose money is under the kitchen table?" instead of just pocketing it. When a father noticed shoes accumulating by the front door, he put his away in the closet, and soon the teen's were not there either. The power of what we do is surprising, but it's natural to observe and be affected by the members of our family. Imitation occurs every day.

Modeling is part of the case *against* punishment as well as an alternative. If a parent uses threats and unpleasant consequences, the young person will also copy the punishing behavior, and become unpleasant to be around. We all try to avoid persons who seem to have critical, punishing ways and yet we imitate them when they are around! Time together becomes unenjoyable and decreases as a result.

A teen developed a problem controlling his anger. He started fights when classmates teased him, and felt bad about himself later. His parents needed to demonstrate and describe their methods of controlling anger in their lives. Mom shared a story: "I was driving to the post office today and when I changed lanes, another driver honked a long time at me. I guess he thought I slowed him down. I felt mad and thought about pulling over and shaking my fist at him. But I said to myself, "I'm angry, but I'm in control—not him. I'm not going to let him make me do something dangerous." Sharing family experiences is an important part of modeling.

Try this modeling exercise. Get family members together to make lists of each other's actions. Each person writes everyone's name, including his/her own, on a piece of paper. Ask each person to list the most positive action of each member of the family after each name. Which persons work hard? Which ones have the most interesting stories, create, dress fashionably, use good manners, tell jokes or funny stories? Add actions that come to mind, but keep them on the positive side. This is not a gripe session.

After everyone has written down a list, exchange sheets and ask someone to read one of the answers on the sheet. Talk over these answers briefly, but move right along to the next person and answer. The idea is to have people think about the positive actions of the ones they live with and encourage these activities. Now, adding the negative behaviors will allow each family member to recognize the moments when they are imitating someone else for good or ill.

The last part of this exercise is a discussion in which people pretend they are other members of the family. Let people choose roles by picking names of family members from a bowl. After the discussion, let people guess who was who. The purpose is merely to see how alike we are and yet how we each have a different view of others. Also, some may gain a clearer understanding of how much of our personalities are a function of those we live with.

"Catch 'em being good" means recognize, praise, or reward the good behavior you see. We all need encouragement to maintain our behaviors, and parents need to show some diligence in catching their opportunities to be encouraging. Teenagers are changing more rapidly than at any other time in life—physically, mentally, socially, and emotionally. They try new behaviors every day to find the adjustment that seems right. Perhaps you remember as a child thinking, "When I make mistakes everyone notices and I get in trouble, but a lot of times I do well, and nobody ever says a thing." To prevent unwanted behaviors, parents need to "catch 'em being good," not just when the desired behavior occurs, but when a behavior in the right direction comes along. Actions that are improvements and steps forward need the most encouragement, recognition, praise, and reward.

For Step 3 you were told the advantages of being realistic about where to start encouraging your teenager. In the "catch 'em being good" alternative, you must also start rewarding at the level the teen can do, and move toward the improvements. A young adult who stays in her room most of the time will not change if criticized, but may come out more often if she finds appreciation and activities she likes when she is in the family areas of the house. What teen can resist sincere praise as when Dad said, "You know that daily log you gave me on my birthday? Today I was thinking how I rely on it every day to keep things straight. It is a tremendous help, thanks to you."

Research tells us that catching people when they come near to appropriate behavior is a more efficient learning technique than punishment for errors. This is because it says, "You've got it! You're on target!" with a wanted behavior. Productive bosses use this. When the boss praises your work you feel certain your actions are right, but when your work is criticized, you can't be sure about how to make it better. Reward says, out of all the possible actions, you found the one I want. Punishment gives less information, because it only says that out of all the possible actions, "Your behavior is one of the many wrong ones!" Considering the many possibilities for error, a teen isn't very much closer to learning an important skill just by being told, "Wrong!".

Which teenager is more likely to learn the important behavior?

1. Teen has no friends. You can
   a) discuss the importance of having friends, or
   b) listen and encourage any socializing in the family and outside it.

2. This young adult pouts and sulks around the kitchen. Would you
   a) tell him to stop being so sour when it's not justified?
   b) ignore pouting and talk pleasantly when the teen acts normal?

3. He/she has no outside interests. You can
   a) require the teen to choose two activities of his/her choice and insist on participation for a half-year, or
   b) you can be available to listen for his/her interests. When the teen wants to do an activity, provide transportation.

In the first example, discussing friendship will be pointedly painful to the teen, but the listening and socializing in the family will provide practice and build confidence for the teen to reach out in other situations. In example two, reactions of anger to pouting will give attention to poor behavior, and possibly encourage it with an argument about its justification. The better plan is to support the less frequent appropriate, pleasant interactions. In the third case about outside interests, both choices are helpful and correct for a teen who needs to develop activities. Insisting on some selections takes authority, but that may be an ingredient needed to get things started.

Making amends is straightening out a mistake or doing a corrected action after unwanted behavior. It is a reaction we often reserve for adults but deny to children. Our reactions to mistakes by fellow adults is to offer help with making amends by providing solutions, not with punishment. Teens deserve the same expectation and treatment.

Remember the movie with the happy ending? The one with a troublesome city teen whose life was popping with mistakes that he could never see coming. His parents punished him, hoping he would avoid future "accidents." At last, in exasperation they sent him to the country to live with relatives. We saw the teen toil the whole afternoon cleaning up a clumsy mistake before supper— making amends. Finally finished, he went into dinner, justified, uncriticized, and with an experience that motivated him to be more careful. Had he been restricted or physically punished, he would have been belittled and lost practice at making things right. Though the movie lesson was unrealistically easy and quick, the message was a good one: the teen learned by making amends, and cleared up his guilt; the adults maintained a healthier relationship with the teen in the bargain.

If you feel at a loss to come up with proper amends when poor behavior occurs, talk it over with the teen. It can be helpful to him/her and you to share ideas at the time. It also relieves guilt when punishment just focuses on the guilty.

Create a three-day diary which shows specific behaviors, punishments, and alternatives you could use. Here's an example:

DAY	UNWANTED BEHAVIOR	PUNISHMENT	BEHAVIOR YOU WANT	MAKE AMENDS BY DOING
Sat. 10 A.M.	Left house before doing chores	Criticized; do chores and extra work; grounded	Do chores before leaving	Do chores and 1 extra. Plan incentives (your *help* if done at the right time)
Sat. 10 A.M.	Curfew violated	Reprimanded; grounded; no telephone use	Be on time or call early next time	Discuss curfew; come in extra early next time
Sun. 2 P.M.	Homework not done	Criticized; can't see TV or friends; do homework	Complete homework	Discuss plan; do homework; spend 1 extra hour studying
Mon. 5 P.M.	Fighting; made hole in wall	Reprimanded and sent to bedroom	Talk and horse around safely	Talk over problem; fix hole together

As you fill your chart, think of the behavior you want. What would you have done if it had occurred instead of the unwanted action? Would you have reacted positively just as you reacted negatively to the error? Was any part of the desired behavior done before the mistakes were made? If so, what encouragement could you give? This chart will be helpful when talking over a behavior with your teen.

Time out means spending a short period of time in a quiet place, alone, after inappropriate behavior. It can be very successful with young teens. The separation of younger teens from others interrupts overheated verbal and physical reactions with a calming-down period. When the teen has regained emotional control she or he can discuss what happened and plan changes. The time period that is most helpful is long enough to break up unwanted behavior and tempers, but short enough for everyone to remember clearly what happened and to want to plan other reactions. Just having time out of a minute or two is effective; a long time out is not necessary.

This alternative cuts off fighting between siblings and helps a parent regain perspective and control, instead of escalating a problem situation. Parents who a try time-out period find it prevents them from using physical and verbal punishments which they regret later. When parents react with punishments they frequently prevent discussion and planning for changes. Because of bad feelings, the bad behavior may occur again. But after time out, each person involved in the problem has a chance to tell his/her feelings and suggestions. The parent and teen can practice the listening and understanding of Step 1, and gain experience planning for a change. Time out sets the stage for a new beginning.

When Mom returned from shopping, she noticed lipstick on the kitchen wall. Mike had been talking on the phone instead of watching his younger sister, Tina, the wall artist.

Mike: But I have to talk on the phone to my friends some-times. It drives me crazy to watch Tina every minute. I shouldn't have to watch her this much! How could she do that! Mom, you've raised her all wrong! I'm not going to clean that up! I have to leave to go to the mall with Bill.

Mom: We're going to have to talk about this.

Mike: I can't stand it! It's not my fault and Tina should have to clean it up! Mom, you can't make me do this!

Mom: Mike, I'm getting mad and you're upset, too. Cool off for five minutes in your room and then we'll put our heads together to work this out (Mike stomps out to his room).

When the two get together, it's likely they will be able to make a compromise on the lipstick art struggle, a lot more likely than if they had fueled their angry feelings a few minutes earlier. Perhaps Mom, Mike, and Tina can do the wall cleaning together. Mike needs some specific activities to do with Tina while on baby-sitting duty, and he can be given extra time with Bill for doing a good job. When you try to reach a solution, if either you or your teen find you can't be reasonable, extend the time out until all persons can contribute to the agreement.

Dad was proud of his intelligent son and daughters, but when the girls fought he couldn't tolerate it. Joy and Bonnie started kidding around and then sparring in the upstairs hall. When a framed picture hit the floor, Dad ran to the stairway and shouted for them to stop. "Joy and Bonnie, you both go to your rooms and we'll discuss this in fifteen minutes, if you're ready to talk reasonably!"

Dad's girls are almost adults; it's time for them to find ways to keep their playfulness from escalating to breaking up the house. Dad's discussion with them as near-equals may make them share responsibility for controlling themselves as they reach for adulthood.

Making rules together means gathering household members to talk over their needs, feelings, and actions and turn them into livable arrangements. When poor teen behavior occurs, such as not doing homework, try out one of the alternatives to punishment discussed earlier. But if the wanted behavior doesn't come and you give it high priority, then it's time to discuss the situation at a family meeting and make a rule together. Teenagers and younger children are very capable of understanding and discussing situations important to their lives and families. Everyone in the household, old enough to participate, should be at the discussion.

Mom and Dad were upset about a call from Greg's math teacher. She said he had not done homework for a week, so the parents focused on planning for a change in the long term. Dad brought up the problem at a family meeting for making rules:

Dad: Greg, your math teacher called to say you need to do your homework. You're getting a deficiency because you haven't done homework for a week.

Greg: That math homework isn't important. I already know how to figure it. My other assignments are the ones I need to do. I can't spend any more time on busy work!

Dad: Greg, we will have to discuss this more, but tonight I want to see your assignment when it's done—before you spend time on other things.

Preparing for the Family Meeting. While Greg did his assignment, Mom and Dad discussed the math homework situation. Before a family discussion, an adult's preliminary session is important to air views and feelings, and in order to form a compromise about the solution. They thought one-half hour of math problems a night was a crucial part of learning to work hard and accurately, and to applying skills to problem solving. During the pre-meeting, adults need to emphasize specific actions, realistic levels of behavior, and practice communication skills they want everyone to use during the meeting.

Greg's reaction to the call gave his parents ideas about ways to support his math work. He needed to be persuaded about the value of math homework, and rewarded for doing it. For persuasion, Mom would tell her story of not wanting to do math homework as a teen, but finally overcoming the math problems one by one.

From practice she found quicker ways to do the work and it became easier. Because she finally succeeded in math, she went on to courses using higher calculations, and eventually, a science career. Greg's parents shared with Greg their belief in the teacher's assignment; she was the expert. They also said that part of earning a living means doing work you don't want to do. Practice at self-discipline enables you to do it. You can imagine Greg's cynical reaction to such philosophy, but it may still ring true and have an influence.

At the preliminary discussion, parents need to explore possible solutions to suggest, in the event that the teen doesn't come up with realistic proposals. What were they already doing to encourage Greg's homework behavior, and what needed to be done? Mom and Dad already used a variety of social and concrete rewards for Greg doing his homework; they played math games, and asked "Greg, what did you learn? Give *us* a problem to solve." At other times they shared math and logic puzzles. They told of ways they applied what he learned to their life situations, to show the value of his skills. After he presented his report card, they celebrated his effort with a special meal.

More concrete rewards for doing math homework were needed. They discussed different options and decided on using points. For every assignment completed, their son could earn points toward a movie or other treat. He may have a better suggestion, but at least they have a positive plan to offer.

The Family Meeting. Young people at a meeting will respect the outcome to the extent they see it taking into account their needs, feelings, and actions. It takes time to listen to every person so allow an ample period. When family members start repeating what others have said, instead of providing new input, you have probably covered the situation. A regular weekly meeting can be helpful to air concerns before they reach the problem stage. The rules and consequences the group agrees on may need reworking later, but be encouraged that practice will improve everyone's skills and productivity. Step 1 concerning communication skills needs plenty of application at these meetings. Also parents should not push for or expect solutions at every meeting.

When Greg has an opportunity to set policy and abide by it, like most teens and younger children, he is likely to take responsibility seriously. Parents need to make clear the importance of the situation in the short and long runs, and follow up with a discussion of adjustments at future meetings. Reasons need to be clearly stated. If parents don't want older brother John to go out with friends more than one night a weekend for several reasons, they need to say so:

"We don't want to have to worry about your safety more than one night a weekend."

"We think studying one weekend night is important."

"And we want you to spend time with the family doing something special some weekends."

All family members need to communicate their views of an event or problem, exploring alternative solutions to a situation, and suggesting a rule and consequence which are reasonable. If parents listen well, the keys to a workable solution can be discovered. Teenagers have a strong sense of fairness, but if teens do not participate appropriately, parents may need to postpone the agreement or set a temporary solution, to be adapted as needed.

An ideal discussion raises issues, explores ways to handle them, and then postpones decisions until everyone has had time to mull over the whole matter. During the interval between sessions, reservations and shortcomings can surface. When a final agreement comes, it will be more realistic because of the added consideration of solutions. More details about making rules and using rewards follow in Step 5.

STEP 5

SUPPORT FAMILY RULES WITH SOCIAL AND CONCRETE INCENTIVES

The first four steps provide guidelines for a positive relationship with your teenager. Your attention to positive communication provides a basis for this relationship. Your focus on specific behaviors helps you evaluate your teen's behavior and decide what to work on. Realistic expectations of your teen will help you encourage actions your teen is capable of doing. Alternatives to punishment keep relationships positive. Now we need some reasonable management of the selection and numbers of rules.

Having a *few important rules* that family members can understand and remember *ensures that errors will be few* and the family atmosphere will be pleasant. We all remember the classroom with too many rules about when to talk, sharpen pencils, put away coats and stand in line (two squares away from the lockers). With so many rules to break, one was always being broken and the teacher did more policing than teaching. The family with too many rules will also have an unpleasant atmosphere, because rules will always need attention and will be broken frequently.

The danger of too many rules makes it worth the parents' trouble to write down any complaint, the specific teen behavior it involves, and reasons why it should change. This will keep the number of rules low and actions to be changed will be selected for their long-range importance and usefulness. Consider the behaviors covered in Chapters 7 and 8 while you are planning rules. The actions include self-worth and care, recreational activities, career plans, part-time job, money management, contributions to the family (in Chapter 7) and schoolwork, social relationships and sexual adjustment (in Chapter 8). Some of these areas have natural outcomes that motivate teens once they get started. Parents can help with that. Step 5 starts a plan by selecting one problem at a time. Let the rest go for now because it's too difficult to plan support for several behaviors at once. List other good and poor actions of your teen to help you decide how important your complaint is in relation to other behaviors. You may decide your complaint is too trivial to worry about and you no longer need to be agitated about it. But if it is an important concern, make a chart that will keep track of the behavior you want.

The Chart. Your chart should show the times of day in order to record when teen behaviors occur. All parents know their teens are moody or tired at certain times, and other behaviors also follow cycles. If a teen is tired after school or in the evening, you might respect that characteristic by avoiding requests until he or she has a more positive outlook. Maximize chances for good behavior by rearranging the schedule for chores, homework, or socializing with the family.

Your chart may give clues to ways you can manage the environment to encourage the actions you want. Parents and teachers know that homework behavior can be improved with some re-arrangement of the surroundings. The PTA's encourage parents to provide a "quiet and private place conducive for homework activities." If Pat needs to eat healthy snacks instead of junk food, have fruit, bread, milk, and vegetables on hand, instead of cookies and soft drinks. Most teens will improve their diets when good selections are available. If Tina needs to be home at 8 P.M., does she have a watch to keep track of time? Are you available to provide transportation if a problem comes up?

If you are concerned about use of time after school before you get home from work, what activities are important to be done? Some possibilities are free time to relax, read, listen to music, watch TV, do cooking, chores or a hobby or activity with a friend at home or at school. You may need to provide more structure by planning ahead with the teen and phoning home.

A Starting Level. Step 3 emphasized a level of behavior that takes into account the teen's present level. Begin chores by asking for some bit of behavior that is so small it is certain to be done. You might request help with one chore before getting down to a card game together. Then, in a planned and announced progression you might ask for additional chores, or more careful completion before each game or TV session. The increasing demands must be small enough to allow a smooth, easy increase in effort. For example, a parent encouraged her daughter, Carrol, who failed her spelling test, to go back to an earlier test she had done well. As she ran through some of that list, Mom noted success, "You sure hold on to them, once you get them!" Then the harder words were mixed in to ensure her practice paid off right away.

How fast can the teenager be moved along? Feedback for the same performance can go stale quickly if you don't move on to support some new and better approximation of the long-range goal. When in doubt, move up your expectation for awhile, but keep in mind that it is all right to go back a step if no opportunity to give support comes along.

When a teen achieves a new behavior, it can be used in a different situation and self-confidence goes up. A young boy who made one meal a week for his family was able to help cook for a spaghetti dinner at school. The family is a nurturing place where learning occurs through practice, and mistakes are accepted. Then, risky steps outward, such as cooking for a school function, are successes which add to self-esteem.

An Exercise—Your Plan for a New Behavior

1. List your complaint and the teen behavior you want, such as "he never takes care of his clothes." Example: My tenth-grader's room is knee-deep in clothes and has not been cleaned in months. I believe in allowing a lot of freedom about room upkeep, but this is unhealthy and ruins the clothes in a few weeks! I think the clothes should be hung

up or put away in the laundry or be washed by the teen, and the room should be dusted and vacuumed.

2. The chart shows when the behavior is to happen. I would like it done on Saturday A.M., but baseball practice is at 10, and Bob likes to sleep until 9. The next choice is Friday after school or Thursday. Discuss the best time with Bob.

3. Can the environment be improved to make the behavior easier for the teen? More hangers can be available for clothes, a clothes rack or hooks can be put in the room, and a bigger chest of drawers for Bob's room. Discuss these choices with Bob. There will be room in the hall clothes hamper for Bob's things. The washer and dryer will be empty for use. The vacuum cleaner will be available.

4. What starting level of behavior can my teen do for immediate success? Bob can hang up all clothes, put them in the hamper, or in the chest at least once a week. Just that should receive a regular positive result, without the clothes washing or the room cleanup.

5. How fast can improvement be made toward the desired behavior? When Bob has had a few rewards for successful weeks of room care, a next step is for Bob to wash his own clothes. (A laundry bag or basket in his room would help.) Then vacuuming can be done once a month. Later, add dusting.

Before planning the last parts of your plan, you will want to read the following sections describing effective social and concrete incentives for your teen's improvements.

Social Consequences. Some family rules are not written, but are part of their accepted norms of behavior. Such norms might be "stick up for your brother and sisters and help each other whenever you can, use good manners, quickly return borrowed items, and listen when others speak." Family members support each other's behaviors without much awareness, by modeling and by social affirmations or rewards such as smiles, nods, encouraging words, gestures, and so on.

Not only was it cold that morning, but Dad was later than usual because at the last minute John had needed some help with home-work. Rushing to snatch up the things he needed for work, Dad hit the winter air with dread of the cold plastic car seats. As he went to the car door, John got out of the already-running car, which was warm and ready to roll. "Hey, thanks, Bud! Nothing like a warm car to start things off right!"

"Well, I know you're late because of me."

"Well, thanks for the warm-up."

Not all good reactions are as obviously and carefully conveyed as this, but when Dad's appreciations are frequent they can turn the course of a relationship as well as provide an example of the family norms. You are trying to create an expectation in your teen, that consistent reactions occur; that family exchanges are usually positive. The reliability is important. A good friend is appreciated not because he says something nice sometimes, but because he is consistently positive.

Reliability can build expectations and habits in negative direc-tions also. A father who reacts to every cough or physical com-plaint of his son on the days following an illness, supports behavior just as surely as when he compliments him for his thoughtfulness about the car. Social rewards are so easy to give that they're used in a very offhand manner, sometimes forgotten when most needed, sometimes thrown in where they build in the wrong direction. Adult attention, support, and encouragement deserve close watching at times. When thinking of a specific teen behavior, consider what behavior *your reactions* are building—for good or ill.

List the parts of the chores to be done.

Support chores and effort with social incentives.

Clear Social Support. Sophisticated adults sometimes give social attention and approval in subtle ways instead of using clear messages. They use nods, the lift of an eyebrow, or curiously phrased remarks: "I should think so!" "You bet!" or "Oh, wouldn't you know!" Adults have a great deal of practice in learning these remarks. The information they convey is learned gradually as a child grows through the teen years, but the young teen hasn't learned all these lessons. Be sure your sophistication doesn't confuse your teen when you are trying to give support for good behavior. Be frank and outspoken when you like what's done. Praise in simple language: "Hey, good job! Great work; that was a super idea!" Say it loudly; say it simply; let teens know you mean it. You have plenty of social support to give, there's no need to conserve it with disguised and half-hearted remarks. It is possible to give too much praise? Yes, but most of us are far from that danger. It's hard to encourage specific good behaviors too much.

At the extreme, too much social support can lose its effect. If every action is praised the teen learns nothing. Your neighbor may always praise his child. In his eyes, the kid can do nothing wrong. Pleasant as this may be, little can be learned from a parent with no standards. In the long run, this kid will encounter some painful lessons in situations where love is not unconditional. At the bottom line a parent's love may be unconditional. But in the moment-to-moment daily reaction, Mom and Dad must show thoughtful selectivity in order to teach.

Concrete Rewards. At times, when parental encouragement by itself is not enough, teens need the traditional motivation of concrete incentives such as money or selective use of privileges (TV time, free time, car time, etc.). Teens need spending money, and love special privileges and watching TV. When they earn these rewards it can add to their feelings of satisfaction. Your teens provide important contributions to family life and their efforts should pay off, but the use of concrete rewards is a controversial procedure.

Giving money to a teen for doing jobs that "should be done anyway" seems to be unnecessary bribery that may build unhealthy expectations. Yet we all expect some benefit for each thing we do, it's just that teens have yet to understand the benefits of many habits such as chores and school work. While they still have much to learn, how do we motivate them?

Adults require concrete rewards for going to work and may even justify household chores and projects as ways of keeping up the house investment. At a workshop, teachers who objected to the use of concrete rewards for teens nevertheless objected to any reduction in training credit they received for the workshop! Students with little understanding of the benefits of education were to learn from these teachers for the love of learning, while the teachers themselves thought *they* deserved increased pay. Teens deserve some opportunity to earn, also.

In addition to the right to some concrete rewards, there is also the need. Teens will have some expenses and parents will provide much of the money. Some of that support should be earned by way of some realistic requests that prepare the teen for future responsibilities.

Teens often need to learn behaviors that require larger amounts of time, energy and self-discipline, and these expectations require concrete rewards. Such bigger actions are the eventual requirements of living an independent and self-sufficient life. They include cleaning a bedroom or parts of the house; mealtime jobs—setting the table, preparing supper, and doing dishes; mowing the lawn and weeding gardens; baby-sitting, and doing homework. These are some candidates for rules supported by concrete incentives, because of the extra effort needed from the teen. If there are only two members in a family, the parent and teenager may be a team, sharing jobs, with low emphasis on rules and concrete payoffs. But earning concrete rewards or special privileges is the fuel that keeps effort coming for big jobs.

An incident of poor teen behavior is often the starter for a rule backed up with concrete rewards. The problem may highlight the need for more than just social encouragement. Yolanda always forgot to take the trash can to the curb, but when she earned fifty cents, she remembered it every time. When Marc earned money for taking care of his much younger brother he was happier than when he was not paid, and his parents felt they could request more conscientious care since he was "hired."

When using "less logical" rewards such as money and TV time, which add to the natural consequences of a behavior, extra planning is required. Agreement can come at the family discussion about the rule and payoff. "You can watch TV only after homework is done. Weekly earnings are paid after chores are done Saturday morning."

Use Social and Concrete Incentives Together. For many habits, the time will come when contrived rewards will be withdrawn and natural benefits, such as social rewards, will have to be enough to continue what has been learned. We reward ourselves for some behaviors we come to value. Until the teen reaches that stage, social rewards will have to be emphasized continually, and given along with concrete benefits, so that practice continues. It's not necessary to hurry your attempt to phase out contrived consequences just because they are unnatural; for example, a few extra dollars a week may be a small price to pay for maintaining home-work behavior.

Activities that other people support and believe to be important are probably the same ones you value—washing the car, mowing the lawn, painting, cooking, shopping for groceries and errands. A concrete incentive such as money or privileges does not have to be large here, because the behavior already has obvious value. A young person usually wants to do these important things; they attract natural approval from others as well as from family. When you allow your teen into your sphere of activities, allow him/her to do the enjoyable (naturally valued) parts as well as the tedious ones. When a young teen washes the car, give her the hose as well as a brush to do the wheels.

Use a Repeatable Incentive. A repeatable consequence eliminates the need for nagging, and the repetition and reminding are done by the consequence. For most of us, now beyond our teens, the rules are rarely tested. We behave the way we do because of accumulated experiences—not all as consistent as parental rules. In the long run a teen will also have to learn from, and adjust to, the irregularities of life's rewards and hard knocks. The rules described here can keep reactions as consistent as possible for learning, before the teen faces all the complications of the adult world. Keep the rules as simple and repeatable as possible without insulting your teen's growing need for adult freedoms.

Sometimes rewards are represented only by symbols others give us: money, certificates, and coupons are examples. Such token rewards may be useful to parents when regular rewards are not available or appropriate because the kids have almost grown up. First, a desired behavior is rewarded immediately by a token, ticket, or point on a chart. Later, the teenager can exchange the token for a previously determined, and mutually understood, reward. The token is money of a sort.

An Exercise—Your Plan for a New Behavior Continues with Incentives

It's time to add convincing reasons and incentives to your behavior-change plan made earlier in this chapter. Your plan already has the first steps: your complaint and the behavior you want from your teen; you have worked out the changes you can make in the new environment so the new action will be more likely to happen than before; you also have the starting level for immediate success that you can expect from your teen, and the gradual improvements you expect In the desired behavior.

1. ***List your reasons for the new behavior.*** Plan your discussion by considering your teen's growing need to control his/her own space. Emphasize reasons for the change that fit your teen's views. What's in it for the teenager? Teenagers see your call to action as merely work unless they can see the benefits. In the example requesting Bob to hang up his clothes, the benefit to clothes care is obvious. That reason is likely to be more important to a teen than safety or cleanliness. Other issues such as, "You'll have a more pleasant room atmosphere," or, "Then you can have friends over," will likely be rejected as invasions of the teen's world. "The family standard" may be emphasized which may help you make few demands and only reasonable ones.

2. ***List concrete incentives for the new behavior.*** Concrete and social incentives need to be added to your plan. Consequences which are closely related to the behavior are most likely to seem logical. Avoid incentives a teen might see as contrived and arbitrary; they probably look like control. For Bob, the parents can deposit $10 a week in a clothes fund, an incentive related to clothes care. Every teen needs new clothes and this way Bob earns them.

3. ***What social incentives do you plan to use?*** Social support for the new behavior must be chosen carefully. Consider your teen's view and observe his/her reactions to find the most effective words. At payoff time, "Great work! Nice work!" are to the point and neutral. For Bob, praise of

clothes he chooses will be appreciated, and the social support needs to come early and often.

A Family Huddle Around Rules and Incentives:

1. Brainstorm your family norms-of-behavior list and include the social supports you use for each item.

2. What rules does your family encourage with concrete rewards?

   Discuss your lists with family members, emphasizing your family's unique systems of norms and rules. Your team members' input is valuable to make your system a winner.

A Short Review Before Step 6. The first five steps of this book form an approach to problems of early adolescents that is practical and yet not difficult to follow day-to-day. The first step, about positive communication style, guides you to talk with your teen in ways that strengthen your ties. You practice reflective and sympathetic statements with your young adult, and avoid evaluation of him/ her. The second step focuses your attention on specific behaviors of your teen to provide you with a clear definition of needs and priorities. Step 3 emphasizes your realistic appraisal of your teen's capabilities, starting there with encouragement, and moving along to behaviors you want. Practice with alternatives to punishment in Step 4 keeps your parent-teen relationship comfortable while working toward desired actions. We see how punishment works against you and your teenager, and we emphasize other choices which work for you both: ignoring, modeling, "catch 'em being good," making amends, time out, and making rules together. The fifth step encourages the habit of positive reactions to speed progress in the right direction: limit the number of family rules, use a chart to pinpoint a problem, set up the home environment to help the behavior you want, and start at a level where the teen can succeed. We see the value of using straightforward social consequences and concrete incentives to achieve improvements.

STEP 6

ENCOURAGE SELF-ESTEEM
AND SUCCESS
FOR BOTH SEXES

Parental expectations of sex differences are revealed in their questions and opinions of teen behavior. Biases can reduce self-confidence of a girl interested in an area traditionally "masculine." It can also delay development of social skills in a boy and discourage him from practicing crucial tasks that could lead to an independent life. Following are some biased questions:

Are you happy?	Are you successful?
Are you acting right?	Did you win?
Is your homework perfect?	Is your homework done?
Is your hair attractive?	Is your hair combed?
Are your shoes shined?	Where are your shoes?
Don't eat too much.	Don't eat too little.
Sleep, you look tired.	Sleep, you act tired.
Exercise to look better.	Exercise to be stronger.
Have friends.	Do sports.
Be friendly. Be attractive.	Be competent. Be productive.

In spite of the recent emphasis on open sex roles, our expectations of boys and girls differ; boys and girls develop different capacities, different motivations, and the world has different expectations of them. Whether or not the characteristics are inborn or learned, there's little doubt that the left-hand column describes our encouragement of girls and the right, boys. We emphasize different values for boys and girls, and different aspects of growing up, partly out of consideration for them and partly out of our desire to prepare them for a world we know still has sexist expectations. Sometimes our emphasis is in the best interest of the child or teen, sometimes not. Parents usually react to a boy by directing him toward success with the tasks at hand and less emphasis on social relationships, but usually we encourage girls to succeed socially and provide only the necessary emphasis on the task at hand. Pushing boys puts on a lot of extra stress concerning the sports or schoolwork, and pushing girls intensifies the social anxieties. If you send messages about what teenagers should do based on their genders, they will be more preoccupied with their roles of being boys or girls than with trying new skills and enjoying their successes.

Encourage Teens to Try New Skills. The job for parents and teachers is to carefully separate fact from prejudice. A teen needs to be encouraged to try many skills, develop interests and abilities into strengths, and enjoy successes. The sources of sex differences are in both the environment and our heredity. There are real differences. Records of school problems with males reflect these different averages for the sexes. Of course, car insurance companies know about these sex differences, too. The parents' role is to avoid unrealistic expectations and unfair limitations created by sex stereotypes and remain alert for opportunities to help teens learn by practice. Taking a risk, trying out new tasks, may be influenced by the teen's self-confidence partly acquired from parents. Sex biases of parents will determine the amount of practice a teen will risk and the chances a teen is willing to take, and in turn, the amount of encouragement a teen experiences.

Encourage a Realistic Self-Concept

"OK," the gym teacher said, "Everybody make two lines at the side of the exercise mats. If you want to practice the standing exercises, get in the line near the windows. To practice handsprings, line up over here."

Donna's friend: "Come on, Donna, I'll help you with the flip."

"Flip?"

"The handspring. C'mon, I'll help you."

"You can get hurt doing that."

"You can get hurt getting off the bus!"

Encourage practice of new activities.

"Naw, it's mostly boys over there. Anyway I'm not very good at that sort of thing."

"OK, but I'm going over. Mr. Effort said I'm getting pretty good for a girl." So Donna's friend went to do handsprings and Donna started for the floor exercises; floor exercises were boring to her, but she felt safe with her own gender, safe from embarrassing mistakes.

Donna's expectations of herself determined what she practiced and her expectation grew from many seeds planted by parents and teachers. There was a choice and she decided to practice merely what she did best—a habit we all have. She was intimidated from trying handsprings perhaps because of adult implications, which may have been realistic. Possibly she has learned from adults and experience that she doesn't have the athletic ability for handsprings and would be hurt trying. Certainly kids have the right to apply their own common sense! But if her timidity came from adult cautions and lowered expectations suggested by the adults merely because she is a girl, she has been tempted away from her potential and another opportunity to gain some self-esteem has been allowed to slip by.

Did Mr. Effort really tell Donna's friend she was pretty good "for a girl?" Or was the sexist qualification assumed by a girl who has become wise to the ways of the world? Whether spoken or presumed, she's a strong person to focus on the encouraging part of the remark and continue her practice.

Let's look at a male example:

> "Today I want you to finish some of the sketches of plants you started outside yesterday." The art teacher starts to visit from desk to desk.
>
> "Hey John, let me have one of your sketches to show Mrs. Aesthetic."
>
> "Use your own, Jim."
>
> "C'mon John, I only need one. I threw mine out when we came in yesterday—I'm no good at this nitty-gritty stuff."
>
> "Do another," John said. "She won't be here for awhile."
>
> "I told you, I'm no good at this nitty-gritty stuff!"
>
> "You don't even try, Jim."
>
> "Oh yeah? I'll see you outside!"

Has a boy like Jim, who says he's no good at "nitty-gritty stuff," been sold on his own weaknesses by a prejudiced society? Is he "no good" because he lacks potential, or is he "no good" because he was convinced to never practice the potential he has?

Encourage Enjoyment of Successes

> Mom and Dad stopped to pick up their two kids from school.
>
> 1st Teenager: "I got my math papers back today, and I got more right than anyone!"

"Wow, that's great. I hope you'll have time this weekend to keep up with the others."

"Oh, I can keep up with them easy." (Does the competitive attitude tell you this person is a boy?)

"Just knuckle down to it and you'll get it."

"I have another decimals assignment tonight."

"Well, if you want to stay at the top, you have to keep at it." (Is this the mother or father?)

2nd Teenager: "Mrs. Brown said we have to choose a final project for home economics, a cooking or sewing project."

Mom: "Cooking can be fun."

"My friend Jennie is doing cooking but I'm better with sewing."

"Wouldn't you rather be with Jennie?"

"I guess you're right."

Regardless of the sexes of these two students, one is encouraged to be concerned with success, while the other is encouraged to be comfortable. Questionnaires about such attitudes tell us that the person in the math class is likely a boy, and the person in home ec is a girl—at least the parents are treating them that way. There is no mistake here, merely an example of common family conversation where parents should be sensitive to their own reactions. Then they can encourage each teen to develop his/her very best potential, without too much concern for fitting common molds.

An Exercise—What Are Your Teen's Interests, Abilities, and Successes?

1. List your teen's interests and abilities so far. Give a few examples of the many areas where time and effort may be spent: school subjects, sports, hobbies—cars, nature, art,

writing, cooking, music, politics; special skills—sociality, organization, and working with younger kids.

2. List ways you can help your teenager have a realistic self-concept about his/her abilities. Recognize your teen's help with plant care, balancing a checkbook, fashion decisions, or child care. "Tom, you definitely have a way with kids. What is it you do that makes them go to you?"

3. On your list, tell how the activities have been encouraged.

   Camping—interest in camping was encouraged by helping her camp out in the backyard and fill out summer camp applications. Finally she was encouraged to plan for a trip with two girlfriends to a local campground.

4. What successes have been enjoyed in each area?

   Bicycle—recognized by friends who asked for help repairing theirs.

   Sociality, math ability, and honesty—encouraged and complimented when he was chosen as treasurer of a school club.

5. Are there any areas your teen has expressed interest in which you limited solely because it didn't fit the usual sex roles?

   Dancing—son wanted to take dancing, but the parent said dancing was a sissy activity. Golf—Judy was interested in golf but Mom said there wouldn't always be someone to go with because not many girls played golf.

6. In what ways can you help extend your teen's abilities?

   Drums—a mother rented a drum set to expand practice time for her daughter. She was able to use her energies to create, rather than to just hang out with friends who allowed few chances to develop creative interests.

Swimming—Dad drove his son and daughter to swim team events even though they were sometimes two hours' distance from home. Both became teen lifeguards the following summer.

The list helps us see the importance of developing a wide range of preferences and potentials which a teen enjoys and does well. The choices a youth feels are successful can be the ones that bloom into a career or lifelong recreation. A listing under item 5 above points to a need for re-evaluation of your decision. The parental role is to avoid limiting the young adult's choices by gender stereotypes, and to encourage the youth to try many activities. The parent can help the teenager realistically see his/her interests and abilities as they develop into strengths. Evaluate activities and purchases which can help your teen strengthen abilities. The goal is discover the largest range of activities possible and for your teen to grow toward independence.

STEP 7

HELP TEENS TO BE USEFUL EARLY

As teens grow they are expected to take added responsibility for their own care. They are expected to learn skills needed to survive as happy, independent adults. They are also expected to contribute to the family. These add up to a lot of requests to make of someone barely beyond childhood. But if we apply the steps of previous chapters, we can help young teens who must deal with all of these demands. The demands often occupy their minds and are sometimes frightening, but they will be less upsetting if teens become gradually more *useful* in their early years.

It is not too soon for teens to practice becoming self-reliant and valuable in helping others. Skills learned now will be useful now and in adult life. The acquired self-esteem gained from new competence and appreciation from others is very important to happiness, and teenagers can begin to learn ways to maintain these good feelings about themselves. Other self-care activities to master include diet, grooming, room care, and social skills. Survival skill success brings rewards in the short and long terms: schoolwork, social and sexual relationships, recreational activities, career plans, part-time jobs, and money management.

Coaching teens about school, social, and sexual relations comes in Step 8. A final area of useful behaviors for teens to practice is family contributions in making decisions, choosing entertainment, and doing the chores. These actions help the family, and prepare teens for future expanded family participation. Encounters with basic problems of adult life provide chances for a new level of understanding and enjoyment between ourselves and our teens, because their concerns are more similar to ours than when they were younger.

Parents Become Coaches

Teens still need a lot of help from their parents, but they need a different delivery system than when they were children. Parents

Practice leads to progress.

need to adjust their parenting styles to their teenagers' growing sensitivities about taking increasing control over their lives, and discovering their own solutions to life's demands, problems, and joys. The parents have fewer consequences to use but more advice to give.

An effective coach spends more time on the sidelines and less in the game, but a coach is a good observer/listener, planner, enabler, storyteller, and model. Observing and listening reveal needs and interests, so a parent-coach can encourage new experiences and ongoing actions. Most new knowledge of the world makes teens see things that should be changed, but they need to know ways to create change. At times teens are optimistic, ready to enjoy moments of life, and set aside responsibilities. They need practice balancing fun with work. Paradoxically, at other times they are pessimistic, less confident in their abilities, and futures, so parent-coaches can help by encouraging teens to practice skills that build bright futures.

The main role of a parent-coach is to enable the teen to learn by doing, to practice as well as listen. For example, Elsa's dad noticed that Elsa spent a lot of time tapping on the table and listening to rock music. She moved around the house a lot, but didn't focus on any satisfying activity. When she mentioned the school band and drums, Dad encouraged her to look into it, talk to the teacher, and learn about what was required. Elsa and Dad went out to get the instrument together. The project involved some parental coaching, some doing on the part of Elsa, and some direct parental help.

When Bryan's school backpack was beyond repair, Mom said he should check around on his own to compare values and prices for a new pack. Then they went together to make a selection—some coaching, some help.

A good coach uses storytelling and companionship as pleasant ways to pass along experiences. Like telling tales around a campfire, stories are less threatening than straightforward advice, and they set out alternatives. Stories make good combinations with doing activities together and the companionship sweetens jobs around the house. Talking over life in the car on the way to teen activities or errands maintains consistency and understanding.

Learning to Improve Self-Esteem

How well does your teenager like himself or herself? Self-esteem is the person's value of self and for every person it is a constant concern. High self-esteem helps a person be happy and productive, and helps to avoid problems such as alcohol and drug abuse, depression, and self-degrading sex.

Does your teen feel loved, unconditionally, by important people in his/her life? Does your teen feel capable of doing things? These feelings are the contributors to self-esteem. We feel success or

Parent as coach.

failure at coping with the world's demands and our ambitions. Teens have less experience than we do and they can reach extreme opinions about themselves, inflated or depressed. Their mood changes can be deeper and are often not as temporary as those of thicker-skinned adults.

We can help teens learn to improve and maintain high self-esteem by our actions. Our most helpful influence is the model we set of feeling good about ourselves. Share your high self-esteem over your own accomplishments and praise your teen every day for his/her strengths and achievements. Encourage your teen to praise his/her own accomplishments and concentrate on the strengths of others. People want to be around those who help them feel worthwhile, happy, and capable. These actions are ones your teen will learn from you. Parents can model good health, personal appearance, setting goals and priorities and your growing-up teen will imitate. The imitation is not always immediate, but how often have you heard a friend say, "I can hardly believe I reacted that way to my kids! It's exactly the way my parents would have done it. I even used the same words!"

Often your example of just being active will be imitated and will be helpful. "Whenever, I feel down, I shoot some baskets." Behavior is therapeutic—if we can get it started. Teens gain satisfaction from doing an activity which interests them: a hobby, a school assignment, or spending time with persons who have common interests. Special experiences can increase satisfaction such as a part-time job and making a career or budget plan. Using these guidelines can help your teenager gain and maintain high self-esteem, the most useful behavior a person can learn. A teen who masters self-care and family duties gains independence and confidence. That teen can risk new experiences.

Teens make decisions on their own.

Mastering Self-Care

Confidence and independence increase when teens assume responsibility for their eating, hygiene, grooming, room care, and language. Teenagers may not like making school lunches at first, but they will feel more capable and grown up when they do the job.

Eating. If a family has not already allowed food choices from balanced offerings at mealtimes, without comment and coercion, teenagers need to have that freedom and responsibility. In the short term they may make poor selections, but presented with healthy choices and using the coaches as models, in the long term teens will eat nutritious foods.

Grooming. Peer pressure usually makes a teen adopt acceptable grooming habits. Choosing unusual hairstyles and clothing may be calls for attention and help, or they may indicate concern for fashion. Within reason, it is probably best not to create confrontation over fashion and style. Does your teen need more attention and support for good behavior? Consider how you would react to an adult visitor: with respect of the individual's grooming choices. When teens assert themselves through unusual clothes and hairdos, parents need to see it as growth toward adulthood. Remember that learning comes through practice with mistakes.

A teen needs to make clothing purchases. This is an opportunity to make and follow a budget. Along with clothes selections comes care. Make a checklist together to specify the parts to be done. The checklist can prevent nagging and provide the payoff.

____ washer load   ____ dryer load   ____ hand wash

Room Care. Sometimes teens love to fix up their rooms to their own tastes and the variety (some would have a less complimentary name for it) is remarkable! Encourage your teen to select his/her own furnishings, as much as possible, with your help with the shopping.

If a young person has gradually learned to pick up clothes, make the bed with a parent, dust, and vacuum, it's time to take over the total job of room care. Social rewards can be very effective, but concrete rewards may be necessary to get the job done.

Before a positive incentive is worked out, parents will have to make an important judgment. How important is a minimum clean up and how often do you want it done? An answer to these "value" questions will lead to an easier decision about how to do the encouragement part. If the request is to be small and infrequent, then just a little support and encouragement might be enough. A major cleaning every week may require something more concrete.

A cleanup checklist spells out the little things, chips away resistance to an all-or-nothing effort, and pays off at an agreed time. What is clean enough for the payoff? The one who has to live with the room the way it is should have the most say. Some allowance should be paid for all parts completed.

Language use is modeled, but extremes picked up from peers or the media can become a habit. Coach Dad told a story from work about his boss losing respect when she used foul words, and Coach Mom told of her soccer teammate who was high on her scale until she used a lot of profanity arguing with their soccer coach. Family members were fond of repeating the remark of a favorite short teacher who stood up to a tall student when he used bad language: "Profanity is a sign of a limited mind."

Learning Adult Survival Skills

Beyond self care, teens are expected to master life skills essential to their happiness and independence during their teen and adult years: schoolwork, social relationships, recreational activities, career plans, part-time jobs, and money management. Help with schoolwork and social relationships will be detailed in Step 8.

Efforts in all these areas will be easier when the teen discovers, "I had lived part of my life before I realized it was a do-it-yourself job!"

Recreational Activities. Teens often complain, "If you can't go out and spend or eat, there's nothing to do!" With many adult physical capabilities and a great deal of information about all the opportunities out there, teens are ready for action and adventure. Chores can fill in some boring moments in a teen's life, but where are the little successes that come from hobbies and recreations?

Teens need help developing satisfaction from their activities. A mom who enjoys tinkering with her car is a model for her teenager as surely as the father who loves knitting sweaters. Encourage a teen to choose two school or community activities, clubs, or pastimes which follow his/her interests. This is a time for the teenager to take control and make choices. You can share cost for fees and supplies, and provide transportation to events. Generosity will pay double dividends when helping a teen learn new interests. Recognize effort and achievement as your teen pursues his/her things!

TV is popular with many teens who look forward to their favorite shows as recreation, an escape from problems or boredom. While relaxing for a half-hour of TV, teens can learn much that is worthwhile. But teens have a tremendous need to develop skills by doing, by interaction with people or things, not by the passive activity of staring. So work with your teen to agree on limits for TV viewing. Be available as a companion to listen and do alternative activities together that you both enjoy. Help your teenager find active interests to replace TV. One family controlled TV time by keeping it off on school afternoons and evenings, unless a parent OK'd turning it on. Teens in that family pursued swim team, soccer, piano, ballet, and raised a seeing-eye dog. The swim team experience led to summertime pool jobs. A lot of parental encouragement and transportation helped those teens start and continue their skill-building hobbies.

An Exercise—Career Interests and Strengths. Psychologists tell us that teenagers who have a career goal are more likely to go on to complete their education and stay clear of drugs, crime, and teen pregnancy than those who have no long-range plan. The goal extends the teen's present interests and abilities and can be changed along the way.

1. Have the teen list his/her ten strongest interests. Examples could be nature, health, music, soccer, computers, work with wood, cooking, helping people, business, politics.

2. Now have the teen list his/her ten strongest abilities. Some choices could be organization, grooming, art, math, reading, understanding others, speedy work, persuading others, working alone, mechanics.

3. Have the teen list five places in the nearby area that have jobs related to each area of interest and strength. Here is an example for music:

library	—	audiovisual librarian
record store	—	clerk
piano store	—	salesperson
pavilion	—	booking agent
school	—	music teacher

These exercises increase teen understanding of themselves and parental understanding of when to praise. Help a teen make a resumé and consider part-time jobs related to his/her areas of interest and strength.

A Part-time Job

Just as hobbies can be therapeutic to a teen, an outside job can fill spare time in a worthwhile way. A job can help a teenager apply learning from home and school, such as ways to get along with a boss and co-workers, organize time and materials, communicate with the public, and be dependable. Seven out of ten jobs filled every day come from grapevine leads, so a teen needs to let people know he/she is seeking a position. Encourage a teen to be selective. Since a teen learns what he/she does, the tasks of a part-time job should be worthwhile. Some positions require too many hours at the wrong times so schoolwork suffers. Others are too isolated and repetitive. An outside job can mean less help with home chores, and less work on charts, and payoffs, so plan to lift some of those requirements when your teen starts a first job. There is bound to be increasing independence, so discuss hours and chores expected, and be extra encouraging for behaviors you agree on. Consider, "What would be fair if I had an adult boarder?" Of course the person would take care of his/her own chores, but would also have special hours, friends, and a job. The teen is reaching for adult responsibility and independence, but still needs your support, coaching, and even limits.

Managing Money

As a teen's allowance or job earnings grow, provide new ways for it to be spent, other than for the teen's own amusement and stomach. Teens can contribute to expenses for birthday gifts and the family car, and start a savings account for a long-range purchase. A matching funds program for buying clothes lets parents and teens share costs, giving a sense of responsibility in selecting clothes and caring for them.

Increase in money from allowance or a job can make your teen into a "fat cat" who sits on his or her cushion with extra money to spend because everything is free. Extra money should create opportunities for teens to expand control and responsibility of their own lives. They can begin to cover their day-to-day expenses, not to just acquire money they spend for special things. It is cruel training to allow a teen to reap family benefits in the household while paying nothing in return. A teen with too much money is a dangerous problem! The teen may have worked for, and have a right to spend the money, but transportation, extra clothes and entertainment should not be free for the rich. For the young teen, however, food and room are part of family sharing and security. They should not be paid for by a teen until he/she completes school and has a full time, self-supporting job.

Teen Contributions to the Family

Parents should gradually expand the teen's responsibility in helping with family decisions, entertainments, and chores. A continuing emphasis on membership in the family confirms the teen's roots and value as a family member.

Sharing decision-making with a teen provides practice with a skill which will have a lifetime of use. Teens have already gained experience in creating family norms, rules and consequences. It is rewarding to them to have a share in planning family purchases, trips, and chores.

How can family members spend time together and yet have everyone get to do something he/she enjoys? A family meeting in advance can help. It can build a little excitement about family outings. Each person should have a say in some aspect of the plans. For example, a trip to a different city might include a side trip selected by each member: visits to a museum, a landmark, a cemetery, a famous store, and a show. A lot of conversation about the choices will add to the anticipation. Instead of passive, backseat passengers, we might have excited learners. Afterward, they will still be talking about each other's choices.

After we get back, how can we split up the family work so everyone shares? Input from everyone makes the plan for work-sharing a winner. Try assignments; then evaluate, and make changes. Enthusiastic cheering and payoffs keep the family members motivated. Some responsibilities for teens might be shopping, putting away groceries, meal preparation and clean up, house cleaning and repairs, yard and car care.

A Teen's Role in the Family Economy

A system of payoffs can compensate teens for contributing to domestic necessities of the family. This part of family life is an economy where members exchange compensation for activities. Psychologists call this exchange system a token economy, because in many early programs tokens were used to represent the payoffs. The traditional allowance is one kind of token economy.

Since some allowance system is an inevitable part of family practice, parents and teens should benefit from an allowance that is based on effort the teen puts toward self and family care each week. You and your teen could agree about chores that need to be done and how much each chore pays. That agreement prevents a teen from timing requests for allowance according to parents' moods.

An Exercise to Plan the Token Economy

1. List the chores you think need to be done each week by your teen. Consider your teen's starting level, need to grow, available time, and family work.

   Examples: a. load of laundry
                    b. clean own room
                    c. wash supper dishes

2. List your teen's weekly/monthly/long-range expenses. Some teens pay for their own school supplies, movies, tapes, and gifts to friends. Others save for big items such as a radio, clothes, a bike, or car.
   a. school supplies $1.00
   b. movie or tape $5.00
   c. other $3.00

3. Place a tentative value on each chore, considering the minimum wage, amount of time your teen takes to do the work, the teen's expenses, and your own generous nature. This is a chance to be encouraging, and fair to the teen and your budget.

Your teen can record work done on a chart or checklist, using an honor system. This is a chance to show trust. As the weeks progress, tallies on the weekly allowance chart will become more numerous and your teen will start saving for shopping. The chart and a payoff time prevent the need for nagging and coercion. When chores are not done by the agreed time, instead of using fines, which undermine confidence in the economy, have the teen make amends, as suggested in Step 4. In this case, "allowance time" should occur with time left in the day for chores to be done if the teen is disappointed in the week's yield.

Points can be used instead of money. When a teen accumulates enough points they can be cashed in for a special treat, a small party for friends, a favorite meal, or an outing. Teens need practice spending and saving money, to learn those skills.

We hear complaints that the token economy uses bribery and over-emphasizes money. It might seem that all the concern for explicit rules about money and how your teenagers get their shares is too detailed and too mechanical. But we all need some compensation for our work and you are paying your teen for work, not bribing to get things done. The label, bribe, takes away respect and the positive emphasis of earning rewards by honest effort which we all enjoy. Always emphasize sincere social rewards, "Well done! Your work helps our family!" so your teen will value his/her accomplishments in addition to the money gained. Teens will be given their shares of family income by some means or another and, as adults, will have to earn their own wages, so they might as well learn gradually to earn their own incomes.

Promotions in the Token Economy

Once the token economy is firmly established, other incentives can be added. The most important of these are promotions based on good performance. This procedure allows for duties on the chart to be changed, improved, and modified as the teen grows up. If the teen performs well on some of the more simple and tedious chores, she/he might be promoted to a better set of duties. Promotions are an important addition to the token economy; they represent improvements in expectation and emphasize a parent's respect for improved capabilities. If no promotions occur in the token economy, then to some extent, that has failed to do what was intended, because the teens are not growing up to new responsibilities.

For example, one mother developed a token-economy program with us by providing an incentive for her son's chores. After the system was applied for several weeks, the son complained that some of the things he was required to do were "kid's stuff." Taking out wastebaskets and garbage sacks were particularly unpleasant tasks for him. A new procedure provided that if he successfully performed the task for fifteen straight days, without reminders from his mother, he would be promoted to a new task, of washing the car. The chart would be changed and the job of removing wastebaskets would be given to his younger brother. The older son looked forward eagerly to this possible change of events because he liked doing anything with the car; the younger son welcomed an

Token economies promote people and responsibilities.

additional task, because he wanted more opportunities to perform duties for tokens from the system.

It's an exciting, challenging time when teens reach for adult privileges and responsibilities. Parents improve their teens' chances for happiness and success as adults by helping them be useful early in the teen years. They gradually master self-care, survival skills, and family contributions. As teens focus more on becoming adults, the teen-parent relationship improves if the parents take on the exciting new challenge of becoming coaches. Coaches listen and observe their teens: Are the teens ready to try a new skill? Do they need special support to attempt a new experience? Coaches plan the list of abilities to be gained gradually, and encourage and request teens to start on those behaviors. Coaches use stories and modeling to strengthen their bonds with teenagers, and point the ways to adulthood.

COACH TEENS ABOUT SCHOOL, SOCIAL, AND SEXUAL BEHAVIORS

Teenagers need guidance to discover and use behaviors that help them learn about school, social, and sexual adjustment. These areas take the most time each day, and if that doesn't include sexual behavior, the preoccupation with the topic earns it a place on this important list. Parents can use their coaching roles to help teens begin using effective study methods, as well as appropriate social and sexual behaviors basic to relationships.

School Behaviors

Sometimes people argue that the performance of good students in present circumstances shows that problem students can shape up also. But we know habits change only for important reasons such as new encouragements for reasonable goals. Threats, reprimands, and coercions are temporary ways to shape up students. But if we could get the poor student consistently going right, he/she would have a good chance of encountering good results and then continuing. We need a way to get that first turnaround to work:

"I like war books," seventh-grader Steven said to the media aide. He always came by to talk to her because she seemed to have time when the regular teachers were busy.

"I know you do, but what about those homework papers you need to do?"

"Oh, I'll never catch up, so why keep trying?"

"Well, I'll give you a reason: for every finished homework paper you show me, I'll find one of those books you're interested in, or I'll have a piece of candy for you. Choose an easy paper first so that you will have some success right away."

This strategy helped Steven catch up in one of his classes, but should candy be used as a reward in school? Shouldn't Steven get the practice of looking up his own books in the media center?

Although these are important points, in this case the need requires concrete rewards in order to get important behavior going again. The use of an easy paper as a starting point was also a good suggestion.

An Exercise—A Classroom Winner!

Counselors coach students to improve their classroom habits with these steps. Use incentives to encourage your teen to try them too.

I. A student influences a teacher's attitude just as a teacher influences a student: When there is a choice, sit in a seat as close to front as possible and keep good eye contact with the teacher during presentations—just as you would practice good listening skills in Step 1, in a private situation.

2. Be alert for a question to ask concerning the material. A continual banter of questions which are unnecessary would do no good, but good questions help learning and teaching.

3. Occasionally talk to the teacher about the subject. On at least a weekly basis speak to the teacher about the class with a question or comparison to some aspect of your other subjects or experiences.

Some people may object to the contrived nature of these suggestions, but many teens have the mistaken notion that the classroom is, or should be, a place where completely passive learning takes place. The student will benefit from an active, assertive role occasionally. The fact is that a classroom is a social situation where exchanges are a part of the learning and the exchanges influence the teacher's grading. Warming your relationship with your teacher will improve your active learning, and *that* will improve grades!

An Exercise—The Questions Game

A Harvard professor always distributes a slip of paper to each student before class. The top line on the slip reads, "The main point of the day was. . ." followed by a space for the student to complete the statement. The next line says, "My question for today is . . ." followed by more writing space. The professor collects the slips each day to see how the main point has been understood and what material is in need of more attention during the next class. Students must think, summarize, and question, and the professor has excellent feedback. Over 100 Harvard professors now use this procedure. Contrived questions do have benefits.

Einstein's mother used to ask him when he came home from school, "Did you ask any good questions today?" If you try to ask good questions in school classes, you have reasons to follow the teachers' presentations, and are more likely to learn than if you have little reason for listening. Use this game at home to practice behaviors your teen needs in school.

1. Explain that you are going to play a question and answer game related to the media and school.

   a. The parent picks a news show, program, or written article heard or seen lately, and makes up a question about the information.

   Example: This morning I read an article about the eclipse tonight. What I want to know is, why does an eclipse happen sometimes and not at other times?

   b. Now, it's the teen's turn to ask a question, about school subject material. Choose classes in which learning needs to be improved.

   Example: What makes clouds change from good weather into rain?

It is not necessary to answer each question, but if this happens, it's a plus toward the goal of the game, which is to focus curiosity on the usefulness of each subject or media item. Repeat the procedure until all school subjects have been covered.

c. A follow-up to the game is for the teen to ask questions in classes at school. Compliment the teen for questions and encourage discussion about the information. If your teen didn't ask a question, have him/her write the ones that would have been best to ask.

Some Tactics for Middle and High School

Studying is a behavior. It has to be encouraged and the performance has to have some form. Sitting and staring at a book is not performance of a behavior and probably results in very little retention; it's boring and hard to keep going.

To get the behavior going with a poor student, we first ask about reading notes. Most students who are failing don't have any. When they study, they stare at things—lecture notes or books—they don't *DO* anything. Most of us don't have the kind of memory that retains a great deal from just looking; it's the *doing* that will be remembered. So I suggest taking reading notes—preferably on cards. For each page of reading the student should take some notes. "Never turn a page without writing something," is the rule.

The reading-note requirement has several advantages. The first is that it becomes a source of motivation because it is a concrete product from which the student can draw a feeling of accomplishment. Second, it is a product that the parent can encourage, review, and use as a basis of other rewards if that's in the plan.

The third and most important advantage is that notes provide benchmarks of progress that allow the student to pick up where he or she left off. It's surprising how much studying is done in small sessions of only a few minutes at a time between interruptions by phone calls, snacks, chores, and people. Without a note-taking habit, most of us start again at about the same place we started before. With past notes, we tend to move on to new material.

A last advantage of active studying comes at review time. A condensation of the work is available that will allow the right material to be memorized, and frantically thrashing through material will not be necessary.

An Exercise—Study Smarter in Class and at Home

1. Try this experiment to find your most effective study method.

    a. Both parent and teen each read silently two different pages from two school texts, trying to remember as much as possible. Then they take a break to listen to 15 minutes of favorite music together while having a snack. After the break, each takes a turn telling everything remembered from the assigned page. The listener needs to take brief notes.

    b. Then both parent and teen read another page of school material *out loud,* trying to remember everything they can. Take a break to do a chore together for about 15 minutes. Then tell each other and take notes about what you each recall.

    c. Now parent and teen should read a page and take notes on what is read. Break for a game of cards. Share what you each remember (without your notes). Each listener takes notes on the material you tell.

Compare the amount of notes from each session. Which study method produced the most recall? Discuss the reasons for your results.

Study smarter: take notes and review them.

Show interest in content, not just teen's performance.

The more activity (reading aloud and taking notes) you do with the study material, the more you learn and remember. Evaluate these study methods and encourage your teen to use the one which works the best for him or her.

Learning Is Useful Now

It's important for parents to provide experiences that point out, here and now, the usefulness of things learned in school. Certainly a ten- or twelve-year-old can balance a checking account for the family, or plan and carry out the family food shopping. This may mean allowing your teen to perform the task before having the tools to do it. For example you may assign your son or daughter the job of balancing the checking account and collecting a "service charge." When he/she sits down to do it, you may hear, "I can't do this because I don't know decimals." Then you can say, "Oh, you need to add decimals! Let me go over that with you. Then you can carry on." Your teen may not enjoy the process of learning decimals, but at least now there is a concrete experience of their importance. The greatest advantage in teaching is having a student with a reason to learn. When the decimals job is done your teen will know that reason.

For school subjects that do not easily apply to daily tasks, parents can influence their teens' respect for the subject by asking questions.

Mom: What was your work in science today?

Ian: We numbered the chambers of the heart and followed a drop of blood through the system.

Mom: I always wanted to know more about that. How does it go through?

Show interest in school projects and point out, from news of the day, where knowledge applies. Parent-teen conversations that bring in schoolwork show the usefulness of the work and improve the teen's self-respect.

The most important guideline comes from early history when Sophocles said, "The learning is in the doing of the thing." If you wanted to improve your tennis, you would probably arrange some time to practice on the courts. If you wanted to learn some new guitar strums, it would take some practice. When it comes to school work it's easy for the student to forget how much practice counts.

Keep a calendar! The calendar should include plans for study time for each day and a record of successes. It should include priorities of the subjects to study so that time is spent on the most important work of the moment. After considering past grades, attendance is the best predictor of grades! Students should be there every day.

Create Payoffs for Practice

Many activities that compete with studying have built-in payoffs, but the benefits of studying are often a long way off. General socializing and boy-girl relationships have obvious immediate pay-offs. Part-time work has an immediate payoff and adds to self-esteem in a more direct way than study time. If Rick Student studies, there are good consequences but they are slow in showing their benefits. For example, the student becomes more efficient as good study skills develop—the longer you practice some behavior the more reliable and useful it becomes. The built-in payoffs for practice include the habit of practice in studying, taking study notes, redoing materials, and keeping a calendar. Future opportunities, grades and preparation for advanced courses and college are all long-range benefits, but are weak motivators for present effort.

So what can a teacher or parent do to reinforce a teen who has not acquired the attitudes or skills to study effectively? While the calendar helps to plan study time, parents need to help in providing a place to study. 1) Provide a place where active notetaking is convenient. This is just as important to the learning place as freedom from distraction. 2) Parents can talk about subjects the students are taking and create examples of the usefulness of the material. 3) Parents reinforce knowledge about the subjects by asking questions—even questions that stump the parents as well as the student and make it necessary to look up the answer in the homework materials. 4) Parents can reinforce and praise *daily and weekly grades* that reflect knowledge learned.

Use Strategies for Tests

Even after students have acquired good study habits through the guidelines of their own practice and encouragement from parents and teachers, they often complain of having trouble with tests. When the students are concerned about a test, they should construct their own version of the test from notes and descriptions given by the instructor. Students often report that more than half of their questions were the same as the ones on the teacher's test! With those questions answered in advance, the students easily remembered their answers and were quickly halfway to a good test grade. They should try out their tests with other students.

During objective tests, answer each question and, for essay tests, answer each question twice. During objective tests certainly every student intends to answer each question, but very often items go unanswered. There are two reasons for this: fear of guessing, and failure to remember the question! The student should carefully read *and eliminate* options. Checking off poor choices allows the student to focus on the remaining options and improve chances that small differences will be discovered. Once an answer has been selected, the student should read the first part of the item one more time to be sure that the selection is actually an answer to this particular question. Very often wrong options are, in themselves, correct, but not the answer to the question.

For essay tests, the guideline is to answer each question twice—once in outline form and then the actual answer. The student should write a brief outline on another sheet before beginning essay answers. This first answer can be in the student's own words and shorthand. For example, in response to the question, "What was important about the Gettysburg Address?", the student might jot down, "Lincoln, at graveyard, during Civil War, trying to unite the country, said country must try hard to finish the war, for equality and people to run government, give quote."

Now, looking at the first answer, the student is likely to make the second answer complete and in good form. Also, as the student is writing the final answer, new points may come to mind to add to the final answer at the right places according to the outline. The grader is more likely to give a high score when the major points are easy to find.

Learning is a required activity of life. Students often believe that if only they could get through school, the demands of learning would be over. Adults know that new learning tasks are always coming up both on the job and at home. The guidelines presented here are helpful at all ages of learning, and students who use them well will not dread the new challenges, but will enjoy new opportunities for success all of their lives.

Social Behaviors: The Art of Liking Others

Most teens worry about how attractive or likeable they are and certainly some primping before an outing can make a difference. However, like all of us, they tend to like people who like them. So it follows that in order to be like*able,* they will have to do some lik*ing.* Cool, moody, critical, sarcastic, angry, or bitter people make interesting characters in movies. But in real life, such characters are not well liked because they take little time to show that they like others! Without making an effort to like others, teens may have uneasy and insecure feelings. At the end of an evening with peers they probably feel they missed something. *Liking is a behavior that bears a message to the receiver,* a communication that must be sent in order for a teen to develop confidence and trust in friends. Consider the following example.

Anne was nervous before John came by for her. When all her adjusting and posturing in front of the mirror was done, the best help would be to plan ways to show she liked John. Physical attractiveness is important, but the other part of being attractive is letting your friend or date know you like him or her. Anne adjusted her hair after the walk to the car and remembered not to slouch when they were riding along. She wondered if he would like her to talk about his football game. Did Anne look at the date from John's side? If she did, she needed to show it by asking John some questions about his activities, family, and job and school work. She probably needs to do some planning of these topics before the next date. If she did like John, she didn't show it because she was preoccupied with herself.

Would you like to be with someone who likes you tonight? John wanted to, but did he think Anne liked him? He didn't know, so he fell into the same mistake Anne was trying to avoid in the first place—worrying about being like*able* when a little lik*ing* would have been a better strategy. How could he have impressed Anne? Tell her about the football game? Drive in a daring way? Tell her about his latest success? Instead, he should have *sent his own liking messages—asking questions about Anne, complimenting her.*

Would Anne go out with him again? Maybe—if she liked him *and* if she thought she was liked! Will he call again? Anne probably thought that it depended on whether he liked her or not. Partly. But it also depended on whether he thought he was liked.

Liking Behaviors and Caring Days

Do your family members use liking behaviors? Then preparing for an outing will not be a stressful time for your teen because he/she understands the basics that make a person likeable. The moments before a party can be planning time: "At the party I want to spend time with . . . . I want to talk to . . . . I will show I like those persons by . . . ." Natural liking behaviors are consistent attention, questions, encouragement, and praise, instead of preoccupation with your own looks and interests. If you do more asking and listening than you do telling, then you're probably on the right track. Liking behaviors are habits that grow with practice and replace their opposites—criticism, sarcastic and negative comments.

Answers are impressive but questions send the messages. A teen asks about her boyfriend's studying; he asks about her day; the messages show concern, they say, "I'm interested in you." In marital counseling a common assignment for both members of the couple is to have "caring days"—days when he or she does a particular thing for his or her spouse—without being asked or expecting to receive anything in return. What do you suppose is the request most often listed for the caring day by the wife? She says, "I wish he would ask me about *my* day." Out of all the things a husband could do, this simple wish is the most common request: personalized interest and attention.

Liking is not always returned, and two-way relationships never balance exactly. One person is always required to go more than halfway to make it work. Socially successful and likeable people put out more than their share of the effort. They go more than halfway and accept relationships that are not ideally balanced in effort. Teens need to live with less than ideal situations at times, and discover when to accept and when to change a relationship, so as not to be unfairly used. Keeping too tight a score on how much you put yourself out for someone may keep things so even that the relationship is not appreciated. "Having a little in the bank" with persons at home or school can help smooth troubles as they come up with those people.

Compliments and questions show that you like others.

Behaviors are attractive

When talking with your teen about some of the reasons for the attractiveness of certain people, look at the behaviors of those people. Teens need to discover that Richard Dreyfuss and Kathleen Turner are attractive for a combination of reasons. Their physical characteristics are not easily copied, but look carefully at the role Richard Dreyfuss played in his romantic scenes. He was concerned, involved, and ready to be a part of his leading lady's solution to problems. John Travolta danced through "Saturday Night Fever" staring into the eyes of his leading lady. Isn't this fantasy? "If he were here, he would be interested in me, too."

When a film wishes to portray the disillusionment of the common fellow who pursues a beautiful and too-sophisticated woman, the script doesn't turn her ugly—just vain, uninterested and not capable of liking others.

Coaching About Sexual Adjustment

A parent-coach can help a teen with sexual adjustment by listening as the teen explores his/her experiences, feelings, and issues, instead of creating fears. Total ignorance of sexual matters is impossible today because of peers and the media. Sex education is an emotional issue, so a parent needs to examine his/her own feelings about it before trying to help a teen. Which topics are you ready to deal with? Dating? Building a serious relationship? Differences between sex drives of girls and boys? Sex before marriage? Contraception? Pregnancy? Disease? Decide what you think is important for your teen to know and do about sex; then prepare to be a listener your teenager can count on.

Teens will decide their own sexual adjustments, but parents have influence. Step away from your own past experiences and feelings about sex and seek what is best for your teen. Besides listening, how can you help? With your teen, discuss a dating policy and stay with it. Coach your son or daughter about dating customs. Explore relationships and topics concerning sexuality with your teen and keep communication flowing.

Create a Dating Policy with Your Teen

Studies link early one-on-one dating, at ages 13–15, to early sexual experiences, before high school graduation. Going out in groups is an alternative some parents use. Talk with parents of other teens for suggestions and support. If your teen belongs to a club or interest group, their activities provide opportunities for outings with the opposite sex, without one-to-one pairings. Few teenagers have the social skills to go it alone for a whole evening of one-on-one dating for 4 or 5 hours, keeping the conversation and activity going well. That's one reason why group dates are best at least until age 16.

Coach about Dating Customs

Since Mom and Dad's courting days, customs have changed some, but your teenager still needs your guidance to achieve successful dates. We've already stressed attention and questions, as rewards between friends that help make dates happy.

A daughter can help make dates successful by being honest: "You choose the show, and I'll choose the snack place for afterwards, but I don't do horror movies!" or "I guess we could go to that movie, but I give it a 6. What do you think of the comedy at the other cinema instead?" Ways to compromise will be learned. Both persons are probably thinking "Act right" and they need to see that the best plan is to let others know what he/she likes, and have a couple of high priority choices handy. When your son or daughter leaves for a date, build confidence with praise for appearance, and wishes for a happy time. Self-confidence is fragile, so no last minute criticism, no parting shots.

Did you have someone to listen when your outing was good and you wanted to share the experience? Or when it was a disaster and you wondered why things went wrong? Your teenager needs a reliable listener. Chances are when he/she comes home to share, it will be a bad time for you to bring up your concerns, *so let other things* wait while teen-listening time goes ahead. Weave in some stories of your own best and worst dates, to strengthen bonds while exploring dating customs.

Your son needs to realize, as old-fashioned as it sounds, that he is still expected to take the lead to plan a successful date. You may be able to help with this when you discuss transportation or car use. A son needs to plan something he enjoys, and ask his date about her preferences.

Set Priorities, Raise Questions and Listen

Parents report success from initial talks with teens when they opened communication lines. The important part, and the hardest part, for the teen, is listening. Parents want to make their case for postponing sex, but the teen can probably only tolerate one point before feeling frustration at being the listener.

With Daughters. Mom brought up building ideal relationships with Joyce while they were walking around the lake. Mom had thought a lot about it and had even written down her ideas. She knew she wouldn't be able to say everything but she had her ideas in mind: that building a relationship of knowledge and trust with someone of the opposite sex takes a lot of time to learn the other person's interests, values, behaviors, goals, and dreams. Trust and commitment increase slowly from small bits of time spent together. The eventual bond of marriage is built on behaviors that show trust and caring.

Mom: What do you want from an ideal relationship with someone of the opposite sex?

Joyce: I don't know. Gee, I guess respect for me and my ideas. Someone who is there for me, someone who likes sports, and has a sense of humor.

Mom: I think respect is real important, too. And trust. I learned to trust your Dad when I saw him every day and we talked between classes, during snacks.

Joyce: You and Dad knew each other less than a year before you were married.

Mom: Yes, but we spent time together everyday talking about our past, present, and future. We came to know the real persons under our co-ed shells.

Joyce: I'll never find a man like Dad! The guys I know don't begin to have it together.

Mom: Men take a long time to grow up.

Joyce: They have a long way to go!

And Joyce does, too. But she has Mom and Dad, to listen and share her journey.

Dad should plan his listening session with Joyce, too. He wants Joyce to understand that when boys have sex they don't always feel commitment, whereas girls often think having sex means commitment. Also, he wants her to realize that contraception before marriage is likely to be used incorrectly, but teens don't like to hear that, because it implies they're not smart. So instead of trying to get across his whole agenda, Dad will try to do something much harder, be a neutral, encouraging listener.

Dad: In your family life class, did you discuss how the sex drive differs between girls and guys?

Joyce: Gosh, we heard more about physical differences than drives. But the teacher did say boys have stronger feelings about sex than girls. Do you think that's right?

Dad: Yes, boys have sex on their minds a lot of the time!

Joyce: Yeah, the boys make so much of it when someone says something even a little bit sexy in class.

Dad: Yes. Guys can be more inconsiderate and selfish than girls about sex. It's good to know that.

If Joyce continues to find a reliable listener in Dad, he may be able to help her understand her own sexual adjustment and the opposite sex.

With Sons. Parents need to keep the lines open with sons as well as daughters. Boys appreciate dads and moms taking time to listen and raise questions to help their sons' sexual adjustments, too. Before Todd had his first serious date alone, he and Dad spent a weekend camping together. Dad noted the important things he wanted Todd to know. If you postpone sex, you get to know the other person better, without the stress, preoccupation and anxiety of a sexual relationship that has no true basis. Waiting means you can both trust each other about sex, and you don't have to hide what you're doing from friends or parents. If you wait for sex you won't have to deal with an unwanted pregnancy, abortion, or disease. The sex drive is very strong, but a short-run need; building a relationship of trust and caring is both a short and long-run need.

Dad: What does a girl want in going out?

Todd: A good time, I guess, and a lot of talking.

Dad: Just to get to know you.

Todd: I guess.

Dad: You talk a lot on dates?

Todd: Yeah.

Dad: Do you ask a lot about her?

Todd: Sometimes. Not much I guess.

Dad: People like someone who asks them about themselves—just like you do.

Dad's on his way to helping Todd learn about relationships by asking questions and letting Todd explore his problem. Todd may even discover that his problem is not lack of sex, but need for companionship and intimacy at many levels.

Keep Communication Flowing

Questions and short stories help keep communication flowing.

Dad: How was the date?

Todd: OK, but Jennifer and I just don't get along very well anymore.

Dad: You're having some rough spots now.

Todd: Yeah, she likes those horror movies. We always seem to do her thing.

Dad: What did she think of your new shirt?

Todd: OK, I guess. She didn't say. Sounds like she doesn't care, doesn't it?

Dad: A little.

Dad's listening helped and when Todd is ready, he'll find someone who cares more.

Questions help teens understand relationships.

Mom: How was the movie last night, Susan?

Susan: Pretty good. Coming out we started talking to Jim and his friends.

Mom: He's a senior, right?

Susan: Yeah, and he comes on strong. They gave us a ride back and he was all over me! He's nice though. I wish he'd ask me out, but he won't unless I, you know, do more.

Mom: I had a boyfriend like that once.

Susan: What did you do?

Mom: Well, not much. I told him where I stood and we got along, but it was a running battle. He'd try something and I'd always put him off. It didn't last long.

Susan: He stopped asking you out?

Mom: Yes, we were both tired of the struggle. I dated a young man who was less aggressive and 'Come-On-Strong' looked for someone more willing.

Susan finds out that Mom went through similar experiences and she feels a little more confident.

Let's look at two more cases, Jane and Todd.

Mom: How was your date last night?

Jane: Oh fine, I guess.

Mom: Just "fine"?

Jane: Tom and I always end up in the same old argument.

Mom: Really? About what?

Jane: Well, you know, like about how far to go.

Up to this point Mom has been pretty neutral and not argumentative. But conversations with teens always have a turning point when the parent signals her intention to be authoritarian, or, sympathetic and helpful. Let's have Mom come up with a question that keeps the conversation in Jane's control.

Mom: What kinds of arguments come up?" (Mom is interested, not angry or opinionated, yet.

Jane: Oh, he says it won't make any problems.

Mom: "No problems?' Just like a man! There are plenty of problems. For example....

Well, Mom has slipped into a lecture mode and Jane is probably moving toward the door, so let's take this one back and replace it with...

Mom: Well, I guess you think there would be some problems. (Again the control of the conversation goes to Jane.)

Jane: Tom thinks there's no problem. Right. For him, maybe!

Mom: Right.

Jane: Yeah, it's no risk for him!

Mom: Being pregnant, you mean.

Jane: Yes!

Mom: Good point.

Now something was said here. Jane's position is stronger and straighter in her mind. No need for closing arguments. Let Mom and Jane walk out in agreement. It's the most we could hope for; extracting a promise would not have as great an influence as Jane's own conviction that she is right. Talk of sex with an open channel for the teen to talk, discover, and state opinions will result in a less confused person who is more likely to make reasonable decisions.

Mom's talk with Jane can expand to the general topic of relationships so that the role of sex for good and bad can be understood. How has it worked out for Jane's other friends? Let's look at a father-son example.

Todd: Girls can be such a pain!

Dad: How so?

Todd: Well, they don't know what they want. They want to go out, but then they get, well, standoffish.

Dad: They don't want to go far enough?

Todd: Well, yeah. It's not like we're doing, you know, everything!

Dad: You don't want to do that?

Todd: Well, I mean I don't expect it.

Dad: Until later.

Todd: Yeah.

Dad: You know that you could get in a lot of trouble with sex.

That's too argumentative. Let's give Dad the same chance we gave Mom. He seemed to get by the choice between authoritarian and helpful at first, but now he's getting ready to lecture. Dad's last remark starts with "you" and it is not hard to figure what's coming. So in Dad's second try let's give him some "it" statements rather than "you" statements. That should provide a little less confrontation and a little more learning.

Dad: It can be a lot of trouble.

Todd: Well, you have to be careful.

Dad: You're right. But I was thinking of the social trouble.

Todd: I don't get it.

Dad: Well, don't people think of sex as a kind of permanent commitment?

> Todd: I guess. That was the problem with Derrick and Karen. When he broke up with her, it was a big argument.
>
> Dad: I guess that's one of the problems. Somctimes sex makes a relationship much deeper for one person than the other. Especially if they barely know each other.
>
> Todd: Well, you should be sure of the relationship.
>
> Dad: It takes time.
>
> Todd: Yeah.

The "lots of trouble" Dad had in mind in the first reaction can now come up by discussing other people, not Todd. For example, how has it gone with Todd's friends, Derrick and Karen? How does the media handle relationships, sex roles, and "trouble"? It can appeal to a teen's occasional negative focus to explore the bias of TV. You hardly ever get a real close look at a venereal disease infection or a diaper change there, and realistic decisions will come from realistic views provided by long, open conversations.

The Media Aids Communication

The popularity of the media with teenagers can be a plus for parents to trigger listening times. When teens and parents watch a TV show together or read the same magazine article, they can talk it over. Ask teens about the situations or characters' actions. Parents need to raise questions, and then, listen, rather than moralize. Listening helps teens express their developing views, instead of being told what to think, which turns them off to the adult and the topic.

When parents recognize the things they do and don't like about the way TV handles sexuality, they may be able to help teens decide their own opinions and feelings. TV and magazines sell products by using material about sex to attract and keep audiences. The media shows sex in favorable ways, while omitting negatives. Sex outside marriage looks joyful on TV, but we are not shown the realistic side: the stress and struggles, the unwanted pregnancy, abortion, and the nine-month stresses of pregnancy without a husband's support. Television rarely shows someone caring for a sick baby, an AIDS patient, or a victim of venereal disease. In a short time span the media cannot possibly cover the eighteen years it takes to raise a person from baby to adulthood, or the lifetime commitment of being a parent. Parents who experience media's omissions with their teens can raise questions about these issues occasionally, and so provide a means to help teens develop their own adjustments to sexuality.

Parents Model Good Relationships

When surveyed, a large number of teens said the thing they wanted most from their parents was for Mom and Dad to really care about each other, to have a good relationship. Teens feel secure when their parents have a close relationship: companionship, attention, encouragement, praise, help, and healthy sexuality. This teaching tool is effective with teenagers—a good model!

STEP 9

PROTECT YOUR FEELINGS
AND YOUR RIGHTS

You have already applied some guidelines for improving interactions with your teenagers. Using Steps 1 through 8, hopefully your communications and relationships with your teen are friendlier, your goals more specific and realistic. Alternatives to punishment and new incentives of Steps 4 and 5 help you focus on opportunities for both sexes. You encourage growth in school and social areas as in Steps 6, 7 and 8.

All of these preceding steps focus on how parental reactions influence teen behavior. The steps require some effort, attention and sacrifice. Most parents are willing to give that effort when it will produce good results, whatever it takes. Parental plans, whether made by the parents themselves or suggested by others, usually give very little consideration to the parents.

This is a serious oversight. Raising a teen is a long process and parents need to be as comfortable with it as possible in order to cope with the long run. Also, what the parents are willing to take will become a tolerance level imitated by their teen. Many mothers hope their daughters and sons will stick up for *themselves* in marriage and the sexist world they enter. Many fathers regret some moments of overreaction and hope for better reactions from their own children. So now, for the benefit of both you *and* your teen we turn the focus on you, the parent.

Teens follow their parents' models

If a parent respects and asserts his/her feelings and rights, then that parent is perceived as a healthy leader the teen can admire and follow. Teenage cries of "Help!" often include accusations that blame parents for the problem: "Mom, the car won't start!" "Dad, where are my shoes? I'm late!" Trying to help with car trouble and lost shoes while meeting work demands, Mom and Dad often overlook their own feelings and rights. When a parent continually sacrifices his/her needs to help others, it is confusing to a teen.

Although it is contradictory to do so, the teen may model the sacrificial and self-deprecating disposition and at the same time be disappointed in the parents. Teens want to emulate someone and the parent, right or wrong, is the most likely person. So the strongest need teenagers have is not for people who provide un-reasonable sacrifice for them, but for models; parents who protect their own feelings and rights while balancing family and work loyalties. Growing teens can learn to apply healthy adjustments to life's demands and joys, if they live with parents who exemplify self-respect as well as helpfulness. So when parents take care of their own needs, they help their teens as well as themselves.

Parents have the right to react when they are not treated with respect and to say "no" when their rights and values are threatened. At times when efforts are not appreciated and inter-actions have soured, moms and dads have the right to express their feelings, think over choices, and change their minds. Parents have the right to make mistakes and still feel good about them-selves. These statements may seem too basic to be emphasized, but many parents need to be reminded of the right to make mis-takes. It is unfair to hold a person to a standard of perfection—parent or teen. With the standard of perfection excluded, one feels a greater freedom to go ahead and try new solutions. Mistakes become evidence of trying something, not evidence of failure. Both parent and teen will find more solutions if their right to make mis-takes is respected.

Many of the rights discussed here were first described in *The Assertive Option* by Patricia Jakubowski and Arthur Lange. Using these rights will provide a protection of your feeling of content-ment in your family, and preserve your spirit for all their teenage years.

1) **You have the right to your own values.**

How much time do you want to put toward cleaning your car? Car care may have low priority on your list and you may have to take some heat from family members who want a cleaner vehicle, less filled with "junk." A parent has the right to spend time in ways that promote his/her own values, the important things in life, as long as others' rights are not denied. So complaints about the poor condition of the car can trigger a plan for a future family activity, but need not make you feel guilty. We cannot let people, even unintentionally, deny the important things in our lives. If your teenager wants to use the car tonight, you may want to make time for a shared session on car care, or suggest that the teen be the one to wash and vacuum the car.

This may help us understand the teenager's resistance to cleaning his/her room. Parents do well to use caution in criticizing a teen's tolerance for clutter and disarray. But good health can be the goal and payoffs the incentives to help a teen learn to value an acceptable standard of room cleanliness.

An Exercise about Values

Have each person in your family list five values they hold and two ways they carry them out in daily life. Pass the lists around and then each person can read the list he/she has, letting others guess who made it.

Some Value Suggestions

achievement	good looks	marriage	power
animals	hobbies	mental health	recreation
beauty	honesty	money	religion
challenge	independence	nature	sexuality
creativity	justice	parenting	social acceptance
environment	learning	peace	sports
friendship	loyalty	possessions	work

The following are examples of values and ways to support them. I value...

1. My family, so I spend time doing activities with them that are fun, and I listen to them tell their experiences and views.
2. Financial security, so I keep money records straight, plan purchases, and keep a budget.
3. Helping others, so I work in education, and support a scholarship program.
4. Physical health, so I exercise regularly, and eat healthy foods.
5. A clean environment, so I recycle and write leaders about it.

2) You have the right to speak out and take action if you are not treated respectfully.

Bill was talking with a group of school friends at the mall when Dad walked by and stopped to be friendly. But after Bill said, "Hi!" he continued his conversation with one friend instead of introducing his father. So Dad introduced himself, shaking hands with each student, and talking to the nearest one. Bob probably realized his mistake when his father took the initiative to make introductions. Later Dad can tell Bill how he felt, so next time his son will remember his responsibility. By taking action Dad showed respect for himself, and set an example of how the situation could be made right.

After Bill loaned his team shirt to his sister, she left it in a heap on the floor of her room. Bill was mad. "If you want to borrow my shirt, show some respect for it! Hang it up and return it when you're done so I'll feel like loaning you other things." Jane knows she was wrong and is more likely to take Bill's comments seriously, because he respected her instead of just demanding the shirt back.

An Exercise about Respect

Each person in your family can write about a situation in which he/she was not respected—not necessarily within the family. Pass the situations to the left several times. Each person can read an example and tell what action he/she would do. How would other family members react? How can we call attention to the need for respect for that person?

3) You have the right to say "no" when your rights are not respected.

Mom was called to canvas the neighborhood for a charity drive. She quickly evaluated her energy limits and answered, "No." Time was short and she realized she couldn't meet commitments to family and work if she took on yet another role. In the past, Mom felt worn out and too tired to do any more, from trying to do everything whenever anyone asked for her help. Later she focused on only the highest priorities, and guarded against trying to do too much. Saying "no" is often so difficult we have to regularly remind ourselves of priorities and rehearse our "no" for that next request which may come today. Family priorities are continuous and can easily slip to a lower place on the list. Parents need to guard against that temptation.

A teen has a right to say "no," also. There was a choice of activities and Laurie knew she would feel sick from the long drive to see an elderly relative; she was able to stay behind by making an alternate plan: visit at a friend's house and take an afternoon bike ride. If the activity was *required,* Mom and Dad could respect her feelings about the car ride by playing *her* radio station and breaking up the trip with meals. If she were old enough, she could drive part of the distance each way.

An Exercise about Priorities

Each family member makes a weekly time plan. An easy schedule to use shows 7 A.M. at the top left side of an 8 x 11 sheet, and the hours can go down the page to 10 P.M. Across the top, list the days. Fill in daily activities and free half-hours.

Now think of one new activity you would say "yes" to, and one you would answer with "no". Share your schedules and activity choices. While some parents resent driving teens to friends' houses or tagging along on shopping trips, some do not. One father enjoyed these opportunities to have time alone with his teenager, confiding feelings, sharing special stories, and building a close relationship.

4) You have the right to feel the way you do, and to express your feelings.

Dad felt down when he came home from work. He'd had a run-in with an associate and other things had not gone well. Instead of trying to turn his feelings around while they ate supper, Mom and his daughters listened to his story without saying he should feel differently. They sat longer than usual around the table as each person pictured the way it was for Dad, and then told about their own day's events. Sharing the way he felt, instead of trying to cover up, helped Dad accept what had happened and look ahead.

Fourteen-year-old Chris complained, "There's nothing to do around here!" Mom felt he was trying to get her to play I-Bet-You-Can't-Make-Me-Happy, but instead of making suggestions, she recognized his feelings, "You sound bored."

"Yes, everyone's sick, and there's nothing I feel like doing."

"With everybody sick, it's hard to find something." Mom saw her teenager making the transition to adulthood, but still looking to her for help with the universal problem of planning one's own time. If

Chris were an adult he might have the same complaint. He had hobbies and chores that could be done, but it would take awhile for him to work out an answer of his own choosing. Numerous suggestions from Mom would probably only continue an unsatisfying game of suggestions, objections, and more suggestions by Mom.

An Exercise about Feelings

Ask each person to share a memory, a time when he/she felt happy, angry, excited, disappointed, or some other emotion, and was accepted for having that feeling. Then share an incident when their feelings were not accepted. How did it make a difference?

5) You have the right to take time to think about choices.

If a parent doesn't take time to consider reactions, a teen may disrupt the family with disturbing announcements: "I'm flunking math!" "I'm quitting band!" "I have to work in Ocean City this summer!" The dramatic announcement could be a way to get into a conversation, or a way to draw attention to a legitimate problem. Waiting for more information may help the parent decide what is really intended. A parent need not react immediately—these are just words, not actions.

A calm approach helps the teen think over the problem. Use listening skills to get the whole story while helping the teen examine details. Parents should hold out for a parent strategy session to find a compromise, instead of allowing teens to play you against each other right there on the spot. If other relatives live with you, enlist their agreement, too, without teens present.

Teenagers benefit, too, from having time to think over consequences before making choices. "Which friend do you want to invite on the camping trip?" "What kind of birthday celebration do you want to have next month?" "What courses will you take next

Take time to consider choices.

Decisions can change as a teen grows.

year?" Given time and choices, teens can learn to take charge of their lives.

An Exercise about Making Choices

List a decision you had to make this past week, and recall how much time you spent considering choices. Did you need more time to make a good decision? How did your choice work out?

6) You have the right to change your mind.

Coaching a growing teenager requires flexibility as the teen's capabilities increase and circumstances change. One family didn't allow sleep-over friends for a long time because their teenager became sick and impossibly grumpy following those occasions. But years had matured their teen so another try seemed only fair.

Parents can remind their son or daughter that parental limits are not the only obstacle to independence and good times. Teens lack education, have restricted job opportunities, and are more limited than just by the rules imposed by parents. But restrictions need to be reduced as a teen demonstrates increasing responsibility and self reliance. A teen presented a reasonable plan to get chores and homework done in order to be able to go on a weekend soccer trip. He convinced his parents to change their negative reaction. In the other direction, parents need not feel bound by an agreement to let a teen do something if they discover later that it would be questionable or unsafe.

A teenager also has a right to change his/her mind. Teens are learning to plan ahead and often find they make more commitments than they can keep. Danny signed up for several clubs and then had to drop out of two activities. When he didn't help with supper because of a club meeting, Dad filled in instead, and Danny made it up the next night.

An Exercise about Changing Your Mind

Encourage family members to share stories. When did they make an agreement and then change it? Have each person tell what happened and how he/she felt about it.

7) You have the right to ask for what you need or want.

As all working folk know, you won't get what you don't ask for. Some parents sacrifice for their teenagers instead of requesting help. Mom wanted assistance unloading and storing groceries, but instead of asking for it, she thought, "My teenagers are tired and I can do this for them." After she finished the work she felt worn out and her sacrificial attitude had turned to resentment. She taught her teens to take advantage of her and she *and they* are likely to pay a price for that.

To help teens enter the world of self-reliant people, we must demand increasingly mature behaviors from them. Instead of nagging them about selecting clothes and being on time, ask them to make their own decisions. They will make mistakes, but they will be on their way to learning. The confidence gained from increased abilities will make the teens feel more adult, better able to have good relationships with you and others. Use allowance and promotions as incentives for behaviors appropriate to the age level.

John wanted help studying for a music test. Dad was just playing solitaire, hoping his son would see he was not busy if help were needed. John felt comfortable asking because Dad often asked him for help, too.

Sometimes when we ask for what we want, we have to be satisfied with none or only part of our goal. But there is still value in asking: it gives everyone information about our feelings and so leads to more honest relationships.

An Exercise about Asking for What You Need or Want

With your family or friends, talk over the right to ask for what you need or want. Have each person think of a time he or she asked or did not ask for help to meet a need or want. How did the experience work out, and how did the person feel about it?

8) You have the right to make mistakes.

Dad forgot to pick up Bryan after a team practice at school. Bryan felt let down and disappointed with his father. When it happened a second time, Dad evaluated his efforts. Lately, work and community activities had been too demanding to allow him to give his son the time he needed. "Everybody makes mistakes, me included," Dad said, "but I'm going to request a replacement on the townhouse committee, drop my racquetball group, and leave work at 4:30 regularly." Mistakes are part of living, but feeling guilty doesn't help us or others. When a slip-up is significant, we can plan a change to make amends.

When her teen acted in ways Mom disliked, Mom started using the adage, "I like you, not your behavior." Then she realized she needed to request certain actions and praise specific behaviors. "I made a mistake by not adding the positive expectation. Now I'm going to try a better way."

Teenagers need to keep mistakes in perspective, too: a burned supper, forgotten chores or school assignments, a thoughtless remark—these are often evidence of a need for raised expectations, requiring practice and incentives.

An Exercise about Mistakes

Ask each family member to share something new he/she is able to do this year, that was not possible last year. Let everyone tell things that made the learning possible, including mistakes.

9)   You have the right to feel good about yourself.

When actions work out well, a teenager happily takes credit, like a player on a winning team, and a parent feels proud, as a winning-team coach. But when bad things happen, parents as well as teens often blame themselves for poor decisions and actions.

The parent must not accept blame and feel guilty for a teen's problems, because the parent has done his/her best and can't be responsible, or have control over, everything the teen does. Many people believe parents are responsible when teens act badly, but teens make most of their own decisions and act on their own most of the time. The responsibility should be passed along with the freedom. Parents, more than their teens, need that occasional reminder.

Parents can set a good example for their teenager by taking on the habit of only accepting credit or blame for their own actions. A teen will learn to accept responsibility for problems as well as successes, if the parent does not accept blame where there is no control. Guide the teen to connect outcomes with his/her own behaviors, not with past parent behavior as a scapegoat.

Parents know a teenager needs to accept his or her own con-sequences, but parent feelings of embarrassment, blame, and guilt can be strong, even if others don't blame Mom or Dad. Those feelings need to be recognized and they can be put to a useful purpose: to analyze problems and plan for changes.

For the happiness of the parent and the family, it's a time for positive steps, to remind everyone of personal and family strengths. Put disappointments in perspective by making lists of things you like about yourself and things you feel proud of. Here are a few examples.

1. I like myself because
    - I work hard; I exercise to stay healthy; I am honest;

- I listen to others; have activities I like to do; and I am faithful.
2. Things I have done that make me feel proud are
   - helped my husband and kids; helped people at work; my drawings; saved money for trips.
3. Ways I have helped my family members are
   - set an example; explored alternatives; listened;
   - kept them company; provided transportation; and helped plan ahead.
4. I feel proud of my family members because they are
   - caring persons; intelligent; honest; and hardworking.

Add an Enjoyable Activity to Your Life

Growing teens will not be available as much as before, but the parent still has a long-lasting, reliable and supportive influence. To feel good about yourself during these years of teen growth toward independence, parents may need to add a new, satisfying activity of their own, or spend more time socializing. The added enjoyable activity or socializing can help a parent who may feel empty, or jealous of the teenager.

Share with Other Parents

During the teen years, parents need friends or supportive people who can discuss common interests and concerns. Parent Teacher Student Association (PTSA) volunteers work together and help each other, by listening and sharing, sometimes in assigned small discussion groups. It is one of the most helpful activities of the PTSAs. Make time to talk with others. They need your companionship, ideas, and solutions as much as you need theirs to feel good about yourself. Your methods of feeling good about yourself will

be picked up by your teenagers. They will learn to accept responsibility for the behaviors they control. They can use lists to keep in
perspective the many aspects of their qualities and achievements.
They can learn the habit of taking action to find satisfying activities
and friends, natural aids to feeling good about themselves.

STEP 10

GIVE SPECIAL ATTENTION TO HABITS CONCERNING ALCOHOL, DRUGS, AND CARS

Steps 1 through 9 can create a strong basis for coaching your teen to avoid drug use and drive a car safely. Each of the guidelines is useful for these challenges. First we will look at ways Steps 1 through 9 can lay a good foundation for those goals. Then we will add a few specific tips to avoid alcohol and drug use and master driving a car.

Step 1 emphasizes listening and talking with your teen in neutral, positive ways. Your time investment helps your teen connect with the family, feel able to solve problems, and enjoy high self-esteem. When communication at family meetings was open, Bob was able to say he was concerned that Dad was drinking too much, and Bob asked him not to. Jill made her request, too. She was to be sixteen soon, and she wanted to take driving lessons at a local driving school because of their emphasis on safety. The family used **Step 2** to choose specific behaviors they could support. After talking over Bob's request, Dad followed through, and Jill signed up for the driving school she wanted. Mom and Dad supplied transportation to her lessons.

Bob's parents used **Step 3** to anticipate, realistically, their son's need to practice handling peer pressure about alcohol and drugs. The family discussed situations and role-played what to say in order to control the pressure. Realistic expectations helped Mom with Jill's first practice drive in an empty parking lot. Jill steered, braked, and turned at manageable paces.

Alternatives to punishment from **Step 4** came through when Bob's basement birthday party took an unplanned turn. Classmates brought forbidden beer, got sick from it, and made a general mess in the bathroom and by the back door. Bob did the major part of the cleanup to make amends. When Jill scraped the family car backing the old Ford out of the carport, Mom and Dad heard the terrible noise. They told Jill how thankful they were she wasn't hurt, but they also denied use of the car for that week.

Step 5 works out family rules with some logical incentives. In Bob's family there is an unwritten family rule: stay healthy by following a proper diet, getting plenty of rest and exercise, and take medication only after natural remedies had been tried. When Bob took a pill for his headache he heard the familiar, "You won't have to take many of those, will you? What are the side effects?" Concerns about taking pills and emphasis on natural health run deep here. Jill kept to family rules for her first trips on her own in the car, in the agreed, familiar area. Mom and Dad encouraged her safety record and she helped them clean the car and check its tires and fluids.

Using guidelines from **Step 6** concerning treating the sexes equally, Bob and Jill's parents celebrated their teens' successes in school, and supported their areas of special strengths, hobbies, and friendships. Dad shared an article he saw about alcohol and drug damage to brain and body cells. "That kind of damage reduces your career choices." Jill's parents pointed to her driving strengths: planning routes for errands and driving defensively. The family discussed news stories of teen car accidents and school suspensions related to drug and liquor use.

When we expect teens to be useful early, as suggested in **Step 7**, they feel important and value their own skills. They are likely to try harder in school work, to help the family that depends on them. Drugs, including alcohol, have little appeal when teens use their time for important activities. Jill sees her mastery of driving as a benefit to her family as well as herself, because she can help with transportation needs.

Step 8 suggests ways to increase teens' growing capabilities in school and social skills. Teens feel increased self-worth from successes with schoolwork and friends. This high feeling of self-worth is one of the strongest deterrents to drug use. When teens do well at school and possess social skills they can keep temptations of dangerous behaviors in perspective.

Parents' feelings about drugs and use of the family car are important as **Step 9** emphasizes. Parents have the right to take corrective action if their wishes are not respected.

Steps 1 through 9 can create a support system for teen success to avoid drug use and master safe driving. We have no magical answers to offer parents to help them keep their teens free from these dangerous behaviors. But when parents ask for steps they can take, we can offer these other coaching strategies they can use to guide their teenagers through the years when they are pressured to use drugs, and begin to drive.

Help Teens Stay out of the Biggest Trouble— ALCOHOL AND DRUGS

While the most dramatic teen-drug stories in the media involve illegal drugs, statistics tell us that your teen is likely to abuse alcohol more than any other dangerous substance. While we list drug symptoms in the next section, the primary attention should be given to the dangers of alcohol abuse. Alcohol abusers are persons whose drinking habits produce excessive absenteeism from work or school, and complaints from friends and family. By the time teens reach college, one quarter are classified as alchohol abusers. Alcohol-related accidents are the biggest killers among 15 to 20-year-olds.

Don't send the message that alcohol is a problem solver. The parent model is one of the best predictors of later drinking habits. Yet families that approve of moderate alcohol use, for example, as in Jewish families where wine is a part of religious services, do not show a greater risk of teenage alcohol abuse. The important factor seems to be the message concerning the role of alcohol consumption. "I've haD a tough day; I need a drink!" is a message that alcohol can solve problems. The message that stress or social inhibitions are helped by alcohol is a part of the foundation of drug dependence. Teens are often tempted to substitute alcohol for lack of social skills. Parents need to set a healthy model of problem-solving based on the school strategies and social practice described in Steps 1 through 9. When teens depend on alcohol to breakdown social inhibitions, the breakdown of sexual inhibitions will quickly become the next bad habit. One of the most common reasons given for unsafe sex by teenagers is intoxication.

Self-Esteem. Increase your teen's self-esteem by spending time together and listening to his/her views and concerns. When parents spend hours with their teens it sends a message, "You mean a lot to me. I care about you." A teen who feels valued and capable is less likely to start taking drugs than a teen who has low self-esteem. Recognize your teen as an increasingly capable, valued family member.

Money. Drug pushers look for teen buyers with extra money, so your teen should carry only the needed amount to school or stores. Listen for information about the amount of money your teen has. Encourage spending money on clothes, the car, personal items, or saving for a goal. Mom helped Tom open a bank account and she drove him to the bank on Friday nights.

Observe. Tune in to your teen's life, habits, and problems. Notice general changes in eating, sleeping, health, and friends.

Checklist 1:
Watch for Changes in Habits

1. Does your teenager need more money than usual, or is money missing from the house?

2. Is your teenager spending more time in his/her room with the door locked?

3. Have sleeping or eating habits changed, or irritability increased?

4. Has your teenager changed friends or become secretive about friends?

Mom liked to eat dinner slowly so she and Bob could talk. It allowed her to monitor his feelings about himself, school, and friends. If Mom saw an unexplained change in his habits she would question him about it and talk with other parents or the school staff.

Talk with Other Parents. Angie's Dad made a point of calling her friends' parents frequently. As a single parent he liked to compare his teen's actions with others'. He liked to keep up on the latest news, but was careful not to tell Angie's secrets because he respected her right to privacy. He knew it was an important part of the trust they shared.

Modeling. Set an example for your teen to follow in the use of tobacco, alcohol, and drugs. Teens usually do as you do, not as you say. Review your habits for the sake of your teen.

Be Informed. As much as you think your teen will never drink, or take drugs, you need to know the signs of use. The following list contains characteristics that all teens have from time to time. Abrupt changes in these characteristics should, however, increase your curiosity and, if you're not satisfied, then you should be suspicious. This is especially true when these changes occur along with changes in the habits listed in Checklist 1.

Checklist 2:
Watch for Changes in Physical Symptoms

1. Lack of concentration; extreme agitation

2. Red, watery eyes; droopy eyelids

3. Runny nose; increased infections and colds
4. Change in sleeping habits—sleeping all day, up all night
5. Slurred or garbled speech, forgetting thoughts or ideas
6. Change in appetite from increase to decrease; cravings for certain foods
7. Change in activity level; fatigue or hyperactivity
8. Change in appearance; becoming sloppy
9. Lack of coordination, clumsiness, falling, or sluggishness
10. Shortness of breath, coughing, peculiar odor to breath and clothes

All teens show some of these characteristics from time to time and it would not necessarily indicate anything about drug use. Any parent of a teen will say that these are characteristics of all teens. The difference that deserves attention is *a cluster of abrupt changes.* "John started going with those older kids last summer and suddenly he didn't care what he looked like; he was sloppy, always sniffing, getting up later and later, and lost interest in every-thing!" The cluster of changes in social habits, attitude, and self-care is enough for a parent to investigate.

Even though you've done your best to help your teen stay clear of alcohol or drug use, you may discover your son/daughter has a problem. Take immediate action to get help from a professional counselor. You can work through the problem together, but it will take support from a person trained to help.

Coach Your Teen to Drive Safely

Mastering use of a car follows the same principles as learning other skills, but your teen places extra value on it. A driving school will help your teen master driving, but you will influence some of the early practice and a great deal of the long-term habits.

At the first driving session with your teenager he/she can simulate driving. Have him/her respond as if starting, braking, and turning the car, to become comfortable with the controls. Talk through a drive around the neighborhood, pretend you accelerate up the hill, pull out around a parked car, and look both ways at the stop sign.

After one or two pretend sessions on the controls, with learning permit in hand, have your teen practice driving in an empty parking lot, to gain real experience with controls and maneuvering the car. Repeat this step several times before moving to the next step. Plan your route each time before starting the car. Most traumatic moments start with a misunderstanding of what was going to be done:

"Turn here!"

"What? Which way?"

"Right here!"

"Right?"

"No, no, left, right here!"

"Left, right, make up your mind!"

The next sound you hear in this situation will not be pleasant, even without an accident. Review plans before taking off.

Now, before our new driver gets the idea all of this is free, set up a matching funds program for gasoline and service for the car, and for the driver's license and insurance fee. For self-esteem, use your new driver's help with errands and family transportation needs.

Driving the Car Is a Useful Incentive

A teen's use of the car is an effective incentive for schoolwork or chores. Work out a plan everyone has a stake in and understands. Earned time can be recorded on the refrigerator door and used as the teen needs it. Instead of taking away earned driving time for poor behavior, use alternatives to punishment. When Jeff didn't do his big English project, Mom and Dad heard about it and *postponed* his car use that week. When he completed the report and was up-to-date in his work, he was able to use his accumulated driving time.

Oversee Driving Practice

When Tom's family traveled to visit relatives in the next state, he did part of the driving, and when Mom or Dad did local errands, Barb was the chauffeur. These teens gained valuable experience and were encouraged for their good driving habits.

It was especially important to practice using appropriate speed. Excessive speed is the cause of most fatal car accidents. After Barb drove Dad to the mall and back, he praised her, "I felt safe with you driving because you kept to the speed limit. Also, when we were stopped at an intersection, I noticed you looked both ways before starting up. So many people run the yellow lights now, a green light doesn't always mean the road will be clear for you."

Mom let Tom know when she felt uneasy about riding with him. "Leave more room between yourself and the next car. What if he had to stop suddenly? We'd crash into him!" Over-balance corrections with praise for your teen's desirable habits, to keep a positive feeling about sharing car rides with you.

In spite of your defensive driving model and encouragement of safety, your teen may use poor driving behavior. Pinpoint a problem and discuss the behavior you want with your teen. Talk over options to encourage the desired behavior but limit the driving privilege until the teen makes a commitment to that goal.

Coach Teens to Find Life's Adventures and Fun

Everyone seeks variety in life, but teens seem to require heavy doses just to keep from falling into depression. "Do you have to do

Teens sharing expenses are more responsible.

something every night? Why is continual entertainment necessary? Can't teens just sit down and relax for a while? No wonder they're so confused—they never take time to think things over!"

The media gives teens romantic notions of all the adventure and excitement passing them by. Teens want a lot of action. They have already developed many adult capabilities and have an amazing amount of energy available. They also have a lot of ideas about the opportunities out there. Instead of satisfaction from everyday events, they seek dramatic happenings to fulfill their needs for action. Adults have discovered the therapeutic effects of mild satisfaction from doing everyday activities: job accomplishments, house- and yardwork, bills and taxes to pay, shopping for a new TV, book, or greeting card. These chores are not the adventurous activities a teenager has in mind, but they do provide satisfaction, and fulfill a need we all have for worthwhile actions.

Activities and Chores Offer Satisfaction. The teen's need to "do something" is not specific. General amount of activity is important. If you have several things you want to do it helps you get through a slow day or week. Activities do not need to be tennis, skiing, movies, or going out with the gang; they can be puttering, shopping, or fixing things. These things never seem to start out as fun, but they do get rid of the blues. Obsessions with music, video games, or TV may be symptoms of needs for expanded personal responsibilities that give personal pride. These entertainments, in moderation, play a useful role to the teen's appetite for excitement in a world with limited opportunities for him or her.

Fourteen-year-old Maya had a big day coming up: she would turn in her social studies project she had worked on for a week, and give a short talk about her project in science. Band was meeting and she would play her trumpet. After school she had to shop for shoes and help make supper. Later she and Dad were going to change the oil in the Ford. Nothing very adventurous, but a schedule of activities she felt good about.

Fifteen-year-old Brent was thinking over his day at school and afterwards: he expected flack for his late reading report; math was confusing because he had skipped the homework for two nights. Even when he was not in trouble at school he had a hard time focusing on his work. After school, his friends were practicing football, but he was ineligible until he raised his grades. His hobbies, biking and mixing music, were on hold until he fixed his bike and radio. At a peak of energy in his life, Brent needs adult help, with repairs, and some incentives to do his schoolwork and chores.

Help Teens Focus on Schoolwork and Chores. When you first suggest an activity to a teenager, you may meet objections. That's when it's time to think of incentives. These are worth it to get things going. We must help a teen start adult chores and focus on important activities such as schoolwork and fulfilling hobbies. If we don't, we can expect complaining and escape to TV and less worthwhile time fillers. Possibly your companionship in the chore would help: do the dishes with me, not for me; work in the yard with me, and shop for groceries with me. As with most problem solving, solutions come from trying numerous alternatives. We adults have learned the activities we like and we enjoy the therapeutic effects. How can we pass along these insights to our teens? Frequent positive feedback for small successes here and now help teens try alternatives and practice important skills.

"Clif, if you show me your completed math and science work you can go to the ice rink with Roger." Mom checks frequently with Clif's teachers to ensure that his work is up-to-date.

Mom had seen so much trouble with Clif and his schoolwork before she insisted he *earn* privileges. After her complaints, he always argued, "When I leave middle school I will do a lot better!"

Not satisfied with promises for the future, Mom insisted that his incentives come as a result of his efforts, not just as freebies. Clif responded to incentives and they helped him focus on important behaviors, and he earned a feeling of pride for his efforts.

Clif's parent is using positive communication to help her son figure out the important things in his life. She tunes in to specific behaviors he can do and she encourages these with companionship and social and concrete incentives. "I'm so proud of the science work you did, Clif!" Regular evening sessions with him, hearing about and helping with his work, and adding incentives, such as allowance and special activities, will bring results. He will make mistakes, but Mom is using alternatives to punishment, such as time out and making amends, to help him see that poor behaviors are part of learning. When they make rules together they talk over concrete incentives Clif wants to achieve, so he feels his efforts are paying off. Mom encourages him to try many activities, to work hard at achieving success, and enjoy the results. Active studying makes Clif learn faster and he enjoys doing things rather than just staring at the book or his notes. He's learning to show he likes his classmates by asking questions about them and listening. Mom sets an example for her son in insisting her feelings and rights are important. She feels all these positive steps will help him say "no" to drug use, and start driving a car successfully in small steps.

All the steps and suggestions in this book take time. Helping a child cross over the teenage years to adulthood requires time—for talking, for planning, and for soul-searching. Talking is for keeping the understanding and the friendship healthy. Planning is for keeping a clear view of the important behaviors and keeping the incentives logical and fair. And the soul-searching is for discovering the times to give over more responsibilities to a growing-up person.

Bibliography

These suggested readings offer additional information about topics covered in the ten steps.

Step 1

1. Faber, Adele and Mazlish Elaine. *How to Talk So Kids Will Listen and Listen So Kids Will Talk.* New York: Avon, 1980.
2. Winn, Marie. *The Plug-In Drug.* New York: Viking, 1985.
3. Carkhuff, Robert R. *The Art of Helping.* Amherst, MA: Human Resource Development Press, 1983.

Step 2

1. Faber, Adele and Mazlish, Elaine. *Siblings Without Rivalry.* New York: W.W. Norton, 1987.
2. Dinkmeyer, Don and McKay, Gary D. *The Parent's Guide, Step/Teen: Systematic Training for Effective Parenting of Teens.* Circle Pines, Minn.: Am. Guidance Service, 1983.

Step 3

1. Bayard, Robert and Bayard, Jean. *How to Deal With Your Acting Up Teenager.* San Jose: California, The Accord Press, 1988.
2. Clarke, Jean Illsley. *Self-Esteem: A Family Affair.* Minneapolis: Winston Press, 1978.

Step 4

1. Gordon, Thomas. *Teaching Children Self-Discipline at Home and at School.* New York: Times Books, 1989.
2. Baldwin, John D. and Baldwin, Janice. *Behavior Principles in Everyday Life.* Englewood Cliffs, N.J.: Prentice Hall, 1981.

Step 5

1. Clarke, Jean Illsley. *Self-Esteem: A Family Affair.* Minneapolis: Winston Press, 1978.

Step 6

1. Gordon, Sal, and Gordon, Judith. *Raising a Child Conservatively in a Sexually Permissive World.* New York: Simon and Schuster, 1983.

Step 7

1. Harris, James M. *You and Your Child's Self-Esteem: Building for the Future.* New York: Carroll and Graf, 1989.
2. Kunjufu, Jawanza. *Developing Positive Self-Images and Discipline in Black Children.* Chicago: African-American Images, 1984.
3. Winn, Marie. *The Plug-In Drug: Television, Children, and the Family.* New York: Viking Penguin, 1985.

Step 8

1. Berla, Nancy; Henderson, Anne T., and Kerewsky, William. *The Middle School Years: A Parent's Handbook.* Columbia, Maryland: National Committee for Citizens in Education, 1989.
2. Goldman, Ronald and Juliette. *Show Me Yours! Understanding Children's Sexuality.* New York: Penguin Books, 1988.
3. Gordon, Sal & Gordon, Judith. *Raising a Child Conservatively in a Sexually Permissive World.* New York Simon & Schuster, 1983.

Step 9

1. Jakubowski, Patricia and Lange, Arthur J. *The Assertive Option: Your Rights and Responsibilities.* Champaign, Illinois: Research Press, 1978.

2. Bayard, Robert and Bayard, Jean. *How to Deal With Your Acting Up Teenager.* San Jose, California: The Accord Press, 1983.

Step 10

1. Baron, Jason D. *Kids and Drugs: A Parent's Handbook of Drug Abuse Prevention and Treatment.* New York. Perigee Books, 1983.

2. American Automobile Association. *Sportsmanlike Driving,* 1987.

Index